At a lunch I encountered Naneke
and have evermore basked in her spell.
History doesn't record
that a partial reward
brought a Rock-ola Juke box as well!

_R._

22 oct '79

# J. KRIVINE

CHARTWELL
BOOKS INC.

## For Sande

I am much indebted to three sources: Roland Gelatt's delightful history of the phonograph, Professor William Pickett's biography of Homer Capehart, and Ken Baxter, whose personal record of the Seeburg company is unique in the industry.

Thanks also to my good friend Simon who suggested the idea of a book, to Janet Sacks who encouraged me and to Aunt Ruth who looked after me in America. David 'Shlok' Slovic and Mike Trussell have given me useful insights and Tim Shackleton has added several of his own to the book.

I am grateful to the following for their good memories: N. Marshall Seeburg II, Fred Mills III, Homer Capehart, Dick Steinberg, Meyer Parkoff, William Smith, David C. Rockola, A. D. Palmer, Mr Carlson, Fred Osborne, J. J. Clement, M. W. Kenney and Mrs McKelvy.

Some of the many people who have helped me out: Mrs Claffy, Studs Terkel, Mart Hallett, Pinko and Diane, Crazy Richard Buescell, R. Brown, Harry McKeown, Paul Oliver, Jo Sanasec, Owen Smith, Martin Brading, Elliot Kaufmann, Jo Goldsmith, Donald Barr, Tessa, Ray and Elexis Cuik Le-Tan.

Plus: the king of the juke boxes, Bob Reno, and the princely Osborn, Rubin, Ward, Plotnik and Ioneri. And a special thank-you to the book's designers, Julian Holland and Julie D. Gross.

Published by Chartwell Books Inc., A Division of Book Sales Inc., 110 Enterprise Avenue, Secaucus, New Jersey 07094

Copyright © J. Krivine 1977

First published in Great Britain by New English Library, Barnard's Inn, Holborn, London EC1N 2JR in 1977.

Printed and bound in Italy by Fratelli Spada, Rome

ISBN O-89009-119-6

# CONTENTS

# INTRODUCTION:
## The Coin Concept

THE COIN machine industry is, broadly speaking, divided into two parts: vending (goods), and amusement (services). The second category comprises games of chance such as one-armed bandits, games of skill such as pinball, and music machines – the juke box.

The coin-operated machine is basically a labour-saving device. It emerged towards the end of the industrial revolution and experienced its most rapid development in the United States where the cost of labour was perceptibly higher than elsewhere. It was also conceived as a means of bringing entertainment within reach of 'the great unwashed'; the coin mechanism is a miniature box-office that harvests the millions of little coins of ordinary folk. These factors alone do not account for the dynamic growth of the 'coin' industry. There is a more elemental force at work which is suggested by this description of an unusual apparatus found in an ancient Eastern temple.

'When the worshipper placed his offering on some portion of the image intended for its reception, the weight of the offering acted on a lever operating a valve in one of the cellars of the temple. This cellar contained a vessel filled with hot water and the action of the valve caused steam to ascend through bamboo tubes to the eyes of the image where it condensed and became transformed into tears. . .

This construction must have required a team of maintenance engineers and in no way could be described as a labour-saving device. Nor do we have any reason to believe that it was patronised exclusively by poor worshippers; on the contrary. What impressed the believer most deeply was the illusion that he himself had caused the image to cry (with gratitude?), thus receiving a personal sign from the deities, and to this extent it was a confidence trick.

The same mystique surrounds the modern coin-operated amusement machine although, of course,

*Romance . . . (Martin Brading)*

on a slightly less metaphysical level. The patron enjoys the fleeting illusion that, by depositing a coin, he is controlling a sophisticated machine and this gives him a feeling of power which is an important component of his gratification. It places him on a one-to-one relationship with the source of the entertainment, rather than being just one of a large audience. The rest of the reward is derived from the novelty of the machine. In the case of the juke box, this is in the styling of the equipment and the constant supply of new records.

The earliest examples of coin-controlled devices in modern times were tobacco dispensers, known as 'honour boxes'. These were found on shop counters in England in the eighteenth century; due to their lack of sophistication, the customer was on his honour to deposit the coin. With the improvements in the standard of engineering in the nineteenth century, this system was superseded by a more cynical device which was able to withhold the rendering of the goods or service until the coin had actually been deposited. Thus the principle of 'pre-payment' (the machine cannot trust people, but people may trust the machine), was established.

The standardisation of the size of the coinage was an important prerequisite to the growth of the industry. In early times while the weight and content of the coin was paramount, size was often erratic. Despite the considerable effort to develop an efficient coin mechanism – as witnessed by the prodigious number of patents – operators agree that it didn't happen until the mid-1930s. Before then the automatic machine was easy prey to slugs (wooden discs, foreign coins, tokens, wire and a variety of tools). Losses to the operators were substantial and this was the principal reason for the retarded development of the vending machines in the early period. Amusement machines (which had no merchandise to lose) were not inhibited by this problem and from the 1890s they were produced and operated in great numbers throughout the United States. As well as being a coin-operated piece of equipment, the juke box is a member of the phonograph family, and the development of the phonograph plays an important part in the history of the juke box.

*Listening to the Edison Automatic Phonograph.* (The Phonogram, *February 1891*)

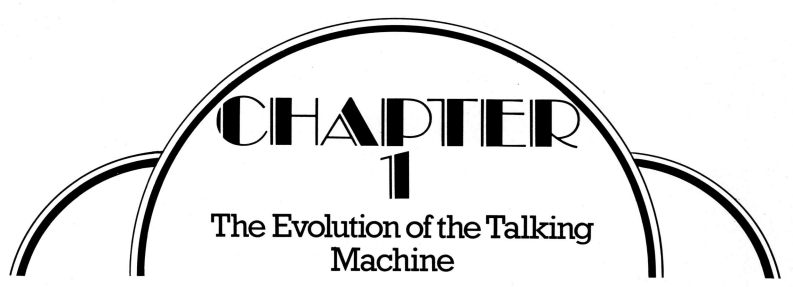

# CHAPTER 1

## The Evolution of the Talking Machine

IF THE origin of the music machine which is the subject of this book is to be traced back to one specific place and time, it would be to a converted barn in Menlo Park, New Jersey, in the year 1877. In this cluttered environment, used as a research laboratory, a thirty-year-old former newsboy and telegraph clerk named Thomas Alva Edison was tinkering around with some pieces of scientific equipment.

'I was engaged upon a machine intended to repeat Morse characters which were recorded on paper by indentations that transformed their message to another circuit when passed under a tracing point, connected to a circuit-closing apparatus. In manipulating this paper, I found that when the indented paper was turned with great swiftness, it gave off a humming noise that resembled human talk heard indistinctly . . . I saw at once that the problem of registering human speech . . . was solved.'

Edison was thrilled by this discovery and immediately dropped the work he was doing on telegraphy in favour of his new brainchild. After a series of tests and calculations he handed a diagram to his mechanic John Kreusi and told him to go ahead and build it.

After four months of trial and error, the apparatus was built. It was the very crudest combination of wheel, feedscrew, stylus, trumpet and diaphragm. Edison sat down before his contraption and uttered the historic words 'Mary had a little lamb'. He reset the stylus, adjusted the machine and again rotated the crank. Sure enough, the rhyme was regurgitated. The sound was much as one might expect from a metallic point being dragged over tinfoil but Edison, admittedly slightly deaf, was delighted. 'I was never so taken aback in my life,' he recalled in later years.

Early in December, and without warning, Edison marched into the offices of *Scientific American* in New York City and proceeded to demonstrate his invention to the assembled group of inquisitive journalists. The machine introduced itself, asked after their health and bade them a cordial goodnight. It was only a short speech but it achieved the desired effect. 'The crowd grew so large that the editor had to call a halt to the demonstration for fear that the floor would collapse' was the

journal's account of the memorable event.

News of Edison's latest achievement spread rapidly throughout the world and the public was consumed with excitement and curiosity. On 24 January 1878 Thomas Edison sold his invention for $10,000 plus a 20% royalty. Evidently he was more interested in the cash than the income, because for the next nine years he turned his back on the phonograph in order to develop the incandescent lamp.

The Edison Speaking Phonograph Company, thus formed, had now to decide what precisely was to be done with its single asset. Edison suggested ten possibilities in an article which appeared in the *North American Review* for June 1878:

'1. Letter writing and all kinds of dictation without the aid of a stenographer.

2. Phonographic book that will speak to blind people without any effort on their part.

3. The teaching of elocution.

4. Reproduction of music.

5. The ''Family Record'' – a registry of sayings, reminiscences etc by members of a family in their own voices and of the last words of a dying person.

6. Music boxes and toys.

7. Clocks that should announce in articulate speech the time for going home, going to meals etc.

8. The preservation of languages by exact reproduction of the manner of pronouncing.

9. Educational purposes, such as preserving the explanations made by a teacher, so that the pupil can refer to them at any moment, and spelling or other lessons placed upon the phonograph for convenience in committing to memory.

10. Connection with the telephone, so as to make that instrument an auxiliary in the transmission of permanent and invaluable records, instead of being the recipient of momentary and fleeting communication.'

However, all those people associated with the phonograph at that time were convinced that the talking machine would take its place alongside the telephone and telegraph essentially as a business communications apparatus; this was where it was needed, and this was where it would earn the most money.

In the meantime, 'the great unwashed' was clamouring to witness the latest scientific wonder. The new company appreciated the importance of public relations and realised that it would take some little time 'to complete the adaptation of this wonderful invention to the practical uses of commerce.' At least they would make some money out of it.

Five hundred phonographs were manufactured and distributed to showmen throughout the United States. As a novelty, the talking machine was superb.

'It would talk in English, Dutch, German, French, Spanish and Hebrew. It would imitate the barking of dogs and the crowing of cocks. It could be made to catch cold and cough and sneeze so believably that physicians in the audience would instinctively begin to write out prescriptions.'

For about six months these machines worked round the clock to keep America amused. The takings, in many cases, were extraordinary. And then, quite suddenly, the public had had enough; they gradually drifted away.

The phonograph was, after all, no more than a mechanical parrot with a very limited repertoire. In 1878-9 it was not suitable for music. A song, for example, was quite out of the question; it would be almost impossible to record, could be played but a few times before it was worn away and the end product would, in any event, be awful.

Edison was deeply hurt to see his invention turned into a fairground sideshow. The national demonstration had, as far as he was concerned, backfired. 'I don't want the phonograph sold for amusement purposes. It is not a toy. I want it sold for business purposes only,' he wrote angrily to his assistant, Tate. The suddenness with which the public had lost interest in the novelty confirmed the view that the future of the talking machine lay in commerce and not in entertainment.

The development work that was being carried out at the Edison Phonograph Company factory had, it seems, come to a standstill. So precocious was the invention that there was no one capable of carrying on Edison's work. The great man himself had put himself under no obligation to work for the company, and in any case, could not now be disturbed. For eight years nothing happened.

In 1883, two scientists, Chichester A. Bell and Charles Sumner Tainter, had started conducting their own experiments on the talking machine and succeeded in substantially improving the quality of the sound by two simple innovations. In the first place, they replaced the tin foil with a cardboard cylinder coated in wax. Secondly, they allowed the stylus to float over the grooves, being held to the cylinder by gravity alone. On 27 June 1885, they applied for patents on their own 'Graphophone'. They raised finance and two years later, the American Graphophone Company was formed with the declared intention of manufacturing and distributing dictation machines to commerce and industry. Edison was not pleased with this development. On the contrary; why couldn't people leave his talking machine alone? There was nothing else for it; he would have to improve his phonograph.

By 1888, although the talking machine, scientifically speaking, was now moving forward, it was a long way from being back in business. A patent war was brewing between the two companies and neither of them had the slightest idea how they would market their products. Help came in the form of one Jesse Lippincott, a Pittsburgh glass magnate who saw a future in talking machines. He succeeded in temporarily unifying the two factions in the interests of science and profit. He entered into an agreement whereby Phonograph and Graphophone were allowed to proceed separately with research and production while he would have sole distribution rights to both products.

Having formed the North American Phonograph Company, he carved the United States into thirty-three territories and allocated the highly desirable distributorships to reputable businessmen. These local companies would rent the talking machines to business establishments within their respective territories for $40 per year. Thereafter, respon-

Edison's original phonograph. (Scientific American, 22 December, 1877)

Early motor-powered graphophone. (Courtesy Roland Gelatt)

sibility for maintenance would be theirs, while the parent company would supply the blank cylinders. The rental would be split fifty-fifty. It seemed like an admirable arrangement.

In selling the talking machine to business establishments the local distributors extolled the virtues of this excellent labour-saving device. The employer could dictate his correspondence rapidly into the machine, which the secretary could play back as she wrote out the letters on her newly invented 'typewriter'. Furthermore the boss could make confidential notes on the cylinder and even keep minutes of board meetings in this manner.

The 'dictaphone' did, however, require no little skill to operate in that the crank had to be rotated at a constant speed. The person speaking into the machine had to speak with particular clarity and more than usual volume. Even then, the reproduction was so crude as to make life quite unpleasant for the typist. In addition, the machines were temperamental and broke down frequently, requiring specialist attention. It would seem that the stenographers who had the unenviable task of deciphering the voice of their employers felt no special attachment for the device. After all, it was their labour that the machines would, in the final analysis, be saving. The reader should not judge it too harshly if occasionally styli were to be gouged through the cylinder, or phonographs dropped on to the uncarpeted floor.

The ingenuity of the machine and the thrill of being in the vanguard of technology pulled the young men of the local companies through some difficult months. Even after they had broken down the resistance of the conservative businessmen in their territories, so unsteady was the machine's performance that many were returned and those that stayed in use required costly maintenance. Take for example Messrs Easton and Cromelin, trained stenographers and, as later events were to demonstrate, first-class salesmen, who had gained the ripest plum of all the territories: Washington DC. They had entire blocks of Government offices (and the Government will buy

anything) not to mention Congress (don't you see, Mr Congressman, now you can leave your memoranda to posterity in your own voice ! ! !) Yet not even this local company made a profit from its operations with business machines. By May 1891, the roster of local companies had been dramatically reduced to nineteen. North American was in extreme difficulties and the courageous Jesse Lippincott suffered a stroke from which he would not recover, but there had been some extremely important developments.

At the second Annual Convention of the National Phonographic Association in May of that year a poll was taken and it was discovered that no less than a third of all operational phonographs and graphophones were actually being used for entertainment. For during the 1880s, the entertainment phonograph had not disappeared completely. In the hands of independent showmen the raucous little machines had continued to grind out farmyard noises and music hall jokes. Now, after 1888, with improvements in the quality and performance of the phonograph, a whole new spectrum of sound entertainment opened up before them.

There was no legitimate means by which they could obtain the new breed of phonograph from the manufacturers, North American, because the local companies had exclusive sales rights in their territories, and in any case, they were not for sale. However, as less enterprising companies began to go under the showmen managed somehow to get hold of much of the equipment, and by 1890, nickel-in-the-slot phonographs were appearing in different parts of the country. We have already noted that by the spring of 1891, many of the local companies had themselves defected to the field of entertainment.

Louis Glass, who had the Pacific Coast franchise, is credited with installing the first-ever coin-operated phonograph in the Palais Royal, San Francisco. The date was 23 November 1889. It had four listening tubes and a coin slot for each tube; it could thus earn as much as 20 cents per play. So successful was this machine, that in May 1891, at the second NPA Annual Convention, he

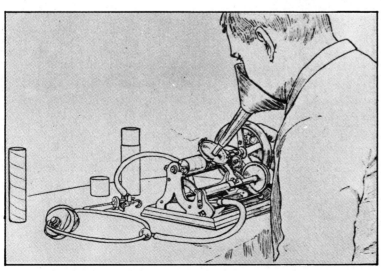

*Talking to the graphophone. (Courtesy* Harper's Weekly)

*Listening to the graphophone. (Courtesy* Harper's Weekly)

*The two latest aids to business. (Courtesy Edison Laboratory National Monument)*

was able to announce that all of his income was now derived from coin operations.

In New York, Felix Gottschalk of the Metropolitan Phonograph Company was also discovering the joys of music. Although he'd seen that coin operations were profitable, he decided to specialise in manufacturing the components for the new amusement machine. In February 1890 the Automatic Phonograph Exhibition Company of New York was established with a capital of $1,000,000. Gottschalk made a deal with North American to supply the components to the local companies on a leasing arrangement.

Fred W. Gaisberg, writing in 1943, recalled a third category of phonograph entrepreneur which surfaced at this time.

'Their purpose was to exploit the phonograph as a dictating machine for office use; however, it proved a failure . . . the company seemed headed for liquidation . . . but was saved by a new field of activity which was created, almost without their knowledge, by showmen at fairs and resorts demanding records of songs and instrumental music.'

Thus the Columbia Phonograph Company became recording specialists in the year 1890.

The Louisiana Phonograph Company reported that one of its machines in a Missouri location had taken $1000 in the two months following April 1891. They were operating fifty phonographs which they serviced twice daily, changing the record each time.

A Mr Amden of Ohio had some sound advice for his fellow-operators who were learning the ropes.

'Cleanliness about the machine and their accessories cannot be enforced too rigidly. The most successful [operators] are those where, in addition to the hearing of good musical [pieces] on the phonograph, the cabinets are kept highly polished, the glass clean, the machines bright, the announcement cards fresh and interesting, the phonograph slot business depends on the patronage of a scrupulous public whom it is well not to offend.

'Receipts increase or decrease in various machines as the records, which are changed daily, are good or mediocre and the different localities require different attractions.'

Whereas ten years ago the public had paid simply to see and hear the phonograph, now they came to listen critically to it. If the machine itself was no longer a novelty, each new phonogram was. It was ludicrous in the extreme to see ten people grouped about a phonograph, each with a tube leading from his ears, grinning and laughing at what he had heard. It was a fine advertisement for the onlookers awaiting their turn.

Events moved very swiftly during the years 1890-4. The injection of a national network of established phonograph enterprises with several thousand machines transformed the coin-operated phonograph from a fairground novelty into a minor industry. The public was responding with great enthusiasm to the appearance of these wonderfully entertaining devices, and the revenues were substantial.

Behind the scenes, however, things were getting very complex.

The corporate structure that Jesse Lippincott had designed for the business machine was quite inappropriate for nickel-in-the-slot phonographs. The local companies had been asking a rental of $40 per annum on a piece of equipment that could earn anything up to $4000 in the same period. The Automatic Exhibition Company of New York was expecting 50% of this income as payment for the supply of equipment which cost no more than $150. The Southern operators were not about to hand over any proportion of their takings unless they had to, and as far as the operators in the west were concerned, it was every man for himself.

In addition, they were being asked to purchase their musical phonograms (cylinders) exclusively from North American. But this was a little unrealistic when one considers that the process of recording was as integral to the phonograph as reproduction; bootlegged records became the norm. Piracy of territory was commonplace, illicit phonograph workshops were everywhere and neither the Automatic Exhibition Company, the local companies nor North American had any way of controlling the activities of the operators. The untimely death of Jesse Lippincott in 1893 deprived the industry of the one man who could have sorted out the mess. The fast money engendered greed and attracted charlatans and con men into the business. By 1894 the industry was in a state of anarchy.

Thomas A. Edison didn't like coin-operated phonographs in 1879, and by 1891 nothing had happened to change his mind. In *The Phonogram* in January of that year he wrote that:

'Those companies who fail to take advantage of every opportunity of pushing the legitimate side of their business, relying only on the profits derived from the coin-in-the-slot, will find too late that they have made a fatal mistake. The coin-in-the-slot device is calculated to injure the phonograph in the opinion of those seeing it only in that form, as it has the appearance of being nothing more than a mere toy and no one would comprehend its value or appreciate its utility as an aid to business men and others for dictation purposes when seeing it only in that form.'

But Edison, as we have already seen, was a realist, and even before he wrote this article, he had begun making musical phonograms at his factory at Orange, New Jersey. Hurt as he was to see his branchild abused in his name, what really rankled was that so little of the enormous profits that the phonograph was now finally earning was coming his way. Thus the East Coast phonograph establishment became alienated to the whole concept of coin-operation and resolved that if they couldn't join it they would beat it.

In 1894, Edison put North American into liquidation. It was a controversial decision at the time, which was to involve him in sixteen years of litigation with the aggrieved local companies, but it was the only way he could wipe the slate clean.

The problem was to find a way of capitalising on the tremendous interest being shown in recorded music. The solution was a phonograph so cheap and so reliable that the public would buy it for their own homes. In 1893 Edison is reported to have said 'I will yet live to see the day that phonographs will be about as common in homes as organs are today.'

In the meantime, Graphophone, his arch-rival, had joined forces with the Columbia outfit under the management of Edward D. Easton and had come to exactly the same conclusion.

---

# CHAPTER 2

## A Nickel in the Slot

IN THE 1890s the coin-operated phonograph was a familiar sight in the United States; the public was developing a taste for recorded music. Their favourite was John Philip Sousa's Marine Band. In 1891 he was signed up by the infant Columbia Phonograph Company and in their catalogue of that year, twenty-seven of his marches were listed. Second in popularity was John Y. At Lee, the famous artistic whistler. Mr At Lee spent his days as a government clerk, his evenings making Columbia recordings in which he sang and whistled an assortment of popular airs. Thirty-six At Lee selections were listed. He was a veritable chartbuster. Comedy also went down well in the phonograph parlours, and two Irish characters had a successful run in the mid-1890s: Russel Hunting created the character 'Casey', and recorded a series that included 'Casey as a Judge', 'The Dying Soldier' and 'The Steamboat', while Dan Kelly, who had signed with the Ohio Phonograph Company, originated 'Pat Brady', and thus 'Pat Brady's Plea in his Own Defence', 'Pat Brady Before an Election' and 'Pat Brady at the World's Fair in Chicago'. It was not at all uncommon, wrote one enthusiast in 1893, to see ladies and gentlemen standing in line before an automatic phonograph in many of the larger American cities to hear him sing and talk. Other favourite performers of the 1890s were George J. Gaskin (pathetic ballads), Dan Quin (musical comedy) and George Johnson (the negro with the infectious laugh), who became famous for his song, 'The Whistling Coon'. By 1894, Columbia was shipping three to five hundred cylinders daily, mostly by mail order.

Because of their unassailable patent position, Phonograph and Graphophone were the sole manufacturers of talking machines and continued

*Pathe's Salon du Phonographie on the Boulevard des Italiens, Paris. (Courtesy Roland Gelatt)*

manufacturing equipment for coin operators well into the 1900s. At that time, the price of an automatic phonograph complete with batteries, ear tubes, blanks and sundries was $190.

Mr Amden, who ran the North American Ohio franchise, was a pioneer of a new type of operation. He saw that if an operator wished to increase his revenue, he had only to purchase two, five or ten more phonographs and place them next to each other in a row. In this way, not only could the operator attend to all his machines at once (they could not safely be left alone for more than half a day) but the public had a whole choice of recordings. In the event, selectivity became a major factor in drawing the public, and 'phonograph parlours' became quite the thing.

Read and Welsh, in *From Tin Foil to Stereo*, describe such an establishment at Vitascope Hall in Buffalo, New York. The vestibule of the theatre was designed to be what was described as 'a palace of pleasure in itself.' Twenty-eight of the latest Edison phonographs were installed for the diversion and instruction of the visitors.

In 1897, phonograph parlours were at their peak of popularity. Most cities in America and Europe had at least one, and the most famous belonged to Pathe in Paris.

'It employed about 40 people. On the spacious street floor there were many desks equipped with listening tubes, with a chair before each desk. There was also a speaking tube at each desk. All the customer had to do was to seat himself, order the selection he wanted played by speaking into the tube, deposit his coin and the record would be played on the phonograph in the room below, which was connected to his particular pair of ear tubes. The customer had a choice of 1500 cylinders.'

It was known as Le Salon du Phonographie. Its equivalent in Milan, The Bar Automatico, provided popular *canzoni* and opera arias could be heard at ten centisima a time.

The parlours were a type of record library; in order to hear the music, you had to sit down and press an earphone to the side of your head. When the tune was over and if you had no more nickels, you got up and left. But the automatic phonograph still could not graduate from the parlours to the restaurants and taverns, at least not until it had been equipped with a horn. And then of course there was the problem of selectivity. You could hardly fill a tavern with trumpeted phonographs; the noise would be unbearable, and there wouldn't be much space to move about in. A satisfactory multi-selection phonograph was not produced until after the turn of the century. The 'Multiphone' was one. It was grotesque in appearance, with a bulging mahogany cabinet and a huge overhead horn concealed behind a grill. The patron would revolve the ferris wheel on which the cylinders were mounted by means of an external crank. He then had to wind the motor to the Edison phonograph, and after all that work he still had to deposit a nickel to hear the tune he had selected. The company went bankrupt in 1908.

The 'Concertophone' of 1906 by the Skelly Manufacturing Company was no more successful. It also demanded a lot of work from the patron – this time manoeuvring a sliding bar – but it featured an important innovation in the Higham Friction Amplifier, which managed to increase the volume of the reproduction. Apparently this was still not loud enough; the company went bankrupt in 1907.

The most significant development in this period from our point of view was the Gabel 'Automatic Entertainer' of 1906. This was a multi-selection phonograph that played discs and represents, technically speaking, the first true juke box. It

was mounted in a five-foot cabinet with a 40in horn on the top. It had a screw-feed mechanism to carry the sound box across the record, a magnetic slug-detector and was wound up from the front by the patron. But Gabel stopped manufacturing the 'Entertainer' in 1908. Attempts to produce an automatic phonograph suitable for the plum tavern and restaurant locations were failing for one reason alone. In the era of acoustic recording the sound from a phonograph was tinny, muffled and accompanied by a pronounced hissing, as the heavy metal stylus was dragged over the surface of the record. If one tried to increase the volume, the hissing would grow to an unacceptable level. It was the sound that was letting the phonograph down.

Roland Gelatt, in his excellent book, *The Fabulous Phonograph*, gives an amusing account of a recording session which illustrated the state of affairs in the 1890s:

'In the centre of a large room are grouped members of Cappa's Seventh Regiment Band of New York; they are surrounded by ten phonographs in a circle, each one equipped with a giant metal horn. An attendant has checked all the batteries and has inserted a fresh wax cylinder in each machine. Now the recording engineer steps before the horn of the first phonograph, starts up the motor, and announces in stentorian tone: " 'My Country 'Tis of Thee' played by Cappa's Seventh Regiment Band, record taken by Charles Marshall, New York City." He stops the motor, steps over to the second phonograph and repeats the same announcement – and so on, through the group of ten. ("A musical record," Mr Marshall believed, "is half made by a perfect announcement. Nothing is more gratifying to a listener to a phonograph than a clear and distinct announcement at the beginning of the record.") When every cylinder has been inscribed with an announcement all ten motors are started up simultaneously. Music pours into the big horns

*Spring-wound nickel-in-the-slot phonograph made in 1900.*
*(Courtesy Edison Laboratory National Monument)*

*Peter Bacigalupi's Kinetoscope, Phonograph and Graphophone Arcade in San Francisco around 1900. Note the linen towels provided to clean the earphones.*
*(Courtesy Smithsonian Institution)*

until each cylinder has received as many sound impressions as it can hold, whereupon Mr Marshall holds up his finger, and the band comes to a full stop at the end of the next musical phrase. If "My Country 'Tis of Thee" has not run its full appointed course, no one seems to worry very much.'

In 1901, a process of moulding cylinders from a master had been invented, although within a few years discs were replacing cylinders as a recording medium. These developments made for more convenience and larger output, but they did little for the quality of the sound. No phonograph could compete with the babble and noise of a busy location, not even the mighty 'Multiphone'. If the phonograph had been the only automatic music available, it might have succeeded. But it was not.

Coin-controlled mechanical music boxes started appearing in the late 1890s. Although as musical entertainment they lacked the range and potential of recorded music, the sound was sharp and loud and, what is more, America grew to like them. By the turn of the century there was a thriving industry and wonderful innovations were being made every year. The 'Peerless Piano', which was introduced in 1908, was so effective and so popular that the automatic phonograph was finally put out of business altogether.

The parlours, once spick and span, had been filling up with novelties like the 'Electric Shocker', kinetoscopes, ball-gum dispensers, popcorn machines and all manner of equipment. Their name now was 'penny arcades' and in 1907 the ghastly arcade itself was being threatened by an even newer novelty, the nickelodeon. The automatic phonograph was overwhelmed.

The phonograph makers had decided in the

Coin-operated 'Multiphone'. (Courtesy C. Y. deKay)

Edison model M nickel-in-the-slot phonograph circa 1900. (Courtesy Oliver Read and Walter L. Welch)

early 1890s to develop the market for home phonographs. They would give Americans recorded music but not so as to benefit the 'coin men'. As the two manufacturers competed for this enormous market, prices went down and the machines improved. Edison's 'Gem' retailed for $7.50 in 1899, thus bringing recorded music within reach of the mass market. The same public that had shown such enthusiasm for the phonograph parlours were now spending their money on their own equipment.

The importance of the coin-operated phonograph in this period was in its role as pioneer. Its success in the early 1890s was responsible for the development and growth of two major industries.

It was the first application of the talking machine to gain any measure of public acceptance and thus gave a vital impetus to the phonograph and recording industries. It also demonstrated for the first time the viability of coin-slot operations and gave a lead to the multitude of musical and novelty machines that subsequently appeared.

The coin-operated phonograph was, in itself, an unremarkable machine. It was, after all, just a phonograph with a coin slot; phonograph historians regard it as a mere adjunct to the home phonograph. Students of 'coin-slot' would point out that, from the standpoint of design and ingenuity, it does not compare with such classics as 'The Caille', the 'Peerless Piano' or an early slot-machine. Sociologically, even at its height it was no more than a national pastime, a novelty of longer-than-average duration. It was equally at home in London or Milan as in Chicago and therefore could not be said to have been an expression of something uniquely American. It made little impact on the technology of the age

*Making violin solo records at the Edison studio.* (Scientific American, *22 December, 1900*)

*Casting and turning blank records at the Edison factory.* (Scientific American, *22 December, 1900*)

# CHAPTER 3

## Coin-operated Phonographs in Eclipse

BY 1908, the public had virtually stopped dropping nickels into automatic phonographs. If it was novelty they wanted, every passing month provided a new coin-operated mechanical wonder. While eating or drinking, there was always the player-piano at hand. When they got home in the evening, they could listen to any song or melody they chose on their very own phonograph.

During this period, the automatic band in its many wonderful manifestations was queen of the taverns. One such machine was a Seeburg 'Solo Orchestrion', located in a roller-skating rink in Des Moines, Iowa.

'We decided to circle the rink once more. We were halfway round the track when it happened – the glorious, magnificent, ear-shattering sound of the biggest, loudest marching band I had ever heard. The sound was coming from a player-piano, a very large one. An elderly man stood next to it listening and adjusting its complicated mechanism. The entire front of the piano had been stripped off and I could see its working parts. The black and white keys depressed themselves and then resumed their positions like magic. The hammers within struck the taut strings firmly and accurately. And its bottom half contained two drums, a bass and a snare playing automatically! Drumsticks, held by unseen hands, beat a sharp tattoo on the snare, another set of sticks clicked out rim shots and a single padded stick thumped the big bass drum, as cymbals clashed.

'Fascinated, I watched the technician go about his task. He put the facade of stained glass in place, placed a clear glass over the percussion section, adjusting things here and there, and lastly pulled the switch that made the variable lights flash on and off. Now there was sound *and* light! My magic piano was whole, my enchantment complete.'

(*Chicago Historical Society*)

This type of instrument was also to be found in the home of many well-to-do American families. If the lady of the house had any reservations about having a 1000lb mechanical band in her living room, the piece of publicity from the Mills Novelty Company shown on p101 would dispel them.

It is worth noting that the Rudolph Wurlitzer Company was also manufacturing this type of equipment. The most successful was the 'Pianorchestra' which combined piano with other instruments. This operated pneumatically from perforated paper rolls and contained from two to seven selections. In addition, it had a very special feature: it could be operated from remote-control wall boxes. In the meantime, changes were taking place in the phonograph industry.

In 1887, Emile Berliner had begun experiments with a machine that played a horizontal disc, but it took him six years of painstaking research before he was ready to put his 'gramophone' on the American market. Berliner's young company had a formidable task. The cylinder phonograph had been accepted as *the* talking machine. The two manufacturing companies were firmly entrenched and developing steadily until at last the phonograph was available to the mass market.

On the other hand, the gramophone had a simpler, more rugged mechanism, was easier to operate, reproduced sound with a marginally greater volume, and, consequently, was better suited for home entertainment. But what finally convinced Berliner and his associates was the simple fact that the records could be stamped out in unlimited batches. Initially Berliner manufactured the records and gramophones on a small scale in the hope of attracting some financial backers. In the autumn of 1895, he found a syndicate of Philadelphia investors who were willing to put up $25,000. The gramophone business, thus established, expanded rapidly, and in 1901 (after a short period of intense litigation), the Victor Talking Machine Company of Camden, New Jersey, was incorporated.

At the end of the first full year of business, Victor had made a profit of almost $1,000,000 and were soon surpassing their phonograph rivals in volume of output. The disc was so superior to the cylinder at this stage (despite the invention of a moulding process for the cylinder in 1901) that in 1902 Graphophone converted its factory to the manufacture of their own version of a disc-playing phonograph.

America was changing in the early decades of the twentieth century. The Protestant ethic that had moulded the country during the rapid expansion of the nineteenth century was giving way to a type of liberalism and this was most pronounced in the big cities. In 1913, a new craze swept the country that was of some benefit to the record companies. *Current Opinion* declared in the autumn of that year that:

'People who have not danced before in 20 years have been dancing during the past summer, afternoons as well as evenings. Up-to-date restaurants provide a dancing floor so that patrons may lose no time while the waiter is changing the plates. Cabaret artists are disappearing except as interludes while people recover their breaths for the following number. One wishes to dance or to watch and to criticise those who dance. . . St Louis was dippy over the new dances, and the sale of a dozen records of this kind to a single customer or to a stranger has not been unusual.'

Tangos, one-steps, hesitation waltzes, Bostons and turkey trots came spewing forth from the record presses. Despite depressed business conditions in the country as a whole, the talking machine industry in 1914 prospered handsomely. Victor's assets jumped from $14m in 1913 to almost $22m by 1915.

There was a far more important musical development at this time. In Victor's supplement of May 1917, there appeared a record, billed as 'the very latest thing in the development of music'. It was a blues and a one-step by a group of white musicians who called themselves The Original Dixieland Jass [sic] Band. They had learnt their music from negro musicians in New Orleans, but were able to present it in a way that went down well with the smart set in New York. This was the beginning of jazz as a 'popular' musical form.

These developments were not welcome in all quarters. Roland Gelatt notes some interesting contemporary observations which are worth repeating. Mrs Marx E. Oberndorfer, National Music Chairman, General Federation of Women's Clubs, put the vital question 'Does Jazz put the sin in syncopation?' and then went on to answer vigorously in the affirmative.

'Jazz [is] that expression of protest against law and order, that Bolshevik element of license, striving for expression in music . . . Dancing to Mozart minuets, Strauss waltzes and Sousa two steps certainly never led to the corset checkroom which holds sway in hotels, clubs and dance halls. Nor would the girl who wore corsets in those days have been dubbed ''Old Ironsides'' and left a disconsolate wallflower in a corner of the ballroom . . . Such music has become an influence for evil.'

According to Fenton T. Bott, a leading light in the American National Association of Masters of Dancing, jazz dancing was a worse evil than the saloon used to be:

'Those moaning saxophones and the rest of the instruments with their broken jerky rhythms make a purely sensual appeal. They call out the low and rowdy instinct . . . Jazz is the very foundation and essence of salacious dancing. The words are often very suggestive, thinly veiling immoral ideas.'

Despite the enormous popularity of the new music, Mrs Oberndorfer and Mr Bott were not, unfortunately alone. The puritans counterattacked; if they couldn't censor music, at least they could attack the root of the wickedness. A powerful backlash was mobilised, and in January 1920, alcohol became illegal and the United States went dry.

If the aim of the Eighteenth Amendment was to purify America, it was not an unmitigated success. Figures for the illicit consumption of booze during the 1920s are not, of course, available, but by all accounts there was plenty about; in fact, quite a few people made a living out of selling it.

During the first two decades of the twentieth century, America had gone on a phonograph binge. According to the US census, total annual sales of phonographs in 1924 amounted to $27,000,000 and by 1919 reached $158,000,000. However, most contemporary observers agreed that, with regard to the quality of the sound, there was some little room for improvement. The industry worked, perhaps, on the principle that 'what the public doesn't know, the public won't miss'. Enormous sums of money were paid in advertising, to persuade a gullible public that each new recording was 'the sweetest, smoothest and most brilliant thing ever heard'. If but a fraction of this income had been spent on serious research, it is possible that the electrification of the phonograph would have arrived sooner than it did.

In the event, it was not until 1919 that AT&T – an organisation not directly involved with phonographs – undertook the necessary research. Joseph P. Maxwell and Henry C. Harrison were in charge of the project; they subjected the science of acoustics to the most rigorous scrutiny, reducing it for the first time to a series of mathematical equations. After much experimentation, they began getting results. By 1924, they had ironed out most of the bugs in the system; it was a real and substantial improvement on anything that had gone before. The frequency range had been extended by two and a half octaves. Bass frequencies never heard before from a phonograph record added body and weight to music. Treble frequencies introduced a definition and detail previously missing; sybilants, for instance, could be heard for the first time. Musicians could now record under more normal and relaxed conditions. But, most important, from our point of view, records could now be played loud.

# CHAPTER 4

## Radio vs Jazz

TOWARDS THE end of the century's second decade, the monopoly that phonographs had on recorded music was coming to an end. In 1919, radio station KDKA, Pittsburg, began regular scheduled broadcasts, first with crystal sets, then 'peanut' (one tube) sets, and finally multi-tube amplifiers that could operate loudspeakers. In 1923 alone, Radio Corporation of America (RCA) made $26 million on the sale of receiver sets. Roland Gelatt writes:

'The radio receiver of 1924, for all the inadequacies of its amplifier and loudspeakers, gave a quality of sound reproduction that the phonograph couldn't even approach. Suddenly, people became aware that machine-made music need not sound tinny, muffled and scratchy.'

From the time when the phonograph makers had first assaulted the home market, they had tried to make into a virtue the fact that the sound became distorted above a certain volume, by promoting the idea that the record player was a quiet and intimate form of entertainment. Radio not only raised the standards of taste in recorded music, but gave the public an opportunity to turn the music up, and they did. At first, the phonograph establishment dismissed radio as a cheap gimmick. Use of 'that word' was forbidden at the Victor factory in Camden. They had grown fat on the enormous profits of the two preceding decades and were impervious to the rapidly changing circumstances of the industry.

When, in 1924, Bell Laboratories invited representatives from Victor to hear the new electrically recorded records and phonographs, Victor's men were not impressed and returned to Camden with an unenthusiastic report. It was not until a year later, when Victor's sales had declined substantially – despite an unprecedented $5,000,000 advertising budget – that they decided to reconsider Bell's offer. As a result of the intro-

*Eddie Cantor broadcasting from KDKA in Pittsburg about 1923. (Courtesy of the Clark Collection, Smithsonian Institution)*

duction of electrical recording and amplification, and, of course, the general economic prosperity, Victor had four more good years with profits running at about $7,500,000 each year. But radio was gathering strength, and the standard of broadcasting was improving rapidly. In 1929, RCA sold 3,750,000 radio sets.

The radio executives were convinced that the phonograph had had its day. To emphasise the point, RCA bought out Victor in 1929, and laid plans for phasing out the phonograph, and converting the entire organisation over to radio. In this venture, they were assisted by the financial disaster of November 1929.

That people now could no longer afford the luxury of a phonograph does not explain the total collapse of the phonograph and record market. Compared to the average 65% drop in the output of consumer durables, records sales slumped by 94% and phonograph sales by 96%. During the 1920s, a handsome 'Panatrope' standing in the parlour, playing the latest records, was a symbol of some degree of prosperity. Now, many of those once-proud owners could barely afford to eat, and the sight of the instrument reminded them not of the good times they'd had, but of the money they had wasted.

According to Gelatt,

'There was . . . a sudden disenchantment on a country-wide scale with phonographs, needles, records and the whole concept of canned music. The malaise broke out in 1929 and spread devastatingly to every city and every state in America. Albums of Red Seal records [Victor's own label], displayed so proudly by a former generation, were unceremoniously relegated to the attic or sold by the pound to the junk dealer. So were the expensive Victrolas on which they had been played.'

A reaction had set in and the phonograph was crushed.

*Billie Holliday recording with a dynamic microphone.*
*(Courtesy Smithsonian Institution)*

*One application of his invention that Edison hadn't*
*considered.*

*Juke (or jook) joint in the South. (Chris Strachwitz/Arhoolie*
*Records)*

What surely won the day so decisively for the radio was the fact that the music was free. Having purchased the radio, one could enjoy an endless stream of entertainment without having to spend another cent, and in 1932, that really counted. The radio men were firmly of the opinion that radio had replaced the phonograph and that there was no going back. But they were overlooking one important attribute of the phonograph that the radio lacked. It enabled the listener to hear exactly what he wanted, when he wanted. In other words, he had complete freedom of choice.

Radio was, broadly speaking, providing the type of entertainment the public wanted; it must cater to the majority of listeners in order to survive. But was this enough? Erik Barnouw, on the subject of broadcasting, describes radio at this time and some of its flaws.

'The impact of radio on musical tastes and consumption patterns was far-reaching but full of contradictions. As musical artists along with comedians, orators and others flocked to the new stations to volunteer their services, the stations began to aspire to an aura of Culture. Live "radio concerts" became frequent, introduced by announcers in tuxedos and stiff shirts. Some stations called their studios their "conservatories". The favoured music was light classical or quasi-classical; one observer called it "potted-palm music". In many cities, hotels acquired radio stations, and nothing was more natural than to use the string quartets that entertained unobtrusively at tea and dinner; such music became a radio staple. Organ music from theatres and department stores (the Wanamaker stores had for some time offered their customers organ recitals), became another radio favourite.

'Focusing on such symbols of culture, most broadcasters of the early 1920s shunned both jazz and country music, which were felt to have no place in a refined atmosphere. Stations that experimented with jazz – WBBM, Chicago, was one of them – were severely criticised for desecrating the air.'

This boycott was directed not only at the music itself, but at the American negro to whom it belonged. But in the 1920s, they were twelve million strong and constituted a sizeable market. Some of the smaller recording companies such as Gennett, Paramount and Sunshine went after it with artists like Jelly Roll Morton, Louis Armstrong, Kid Ory, Billie Holliday and King Oliver. Because radio neglected this area of music, jazz records were the only category that really survived the catastrophic drop in sales in 1930. It is said that Bessie Smith kept Columbia afloat at this time, and likewise, Victor and Brunswick began to emphasise their 'race' products.

In the South, the venue for jazz and blues was the 'juke joint'. The word 'juke' like 'funk' or 'rock 'n' roll' was a synonym for sex, dance and music, a combination that white society strenuously refused to acknowledge. There were shanty bars and cafes in poor agricultural areas where negroes were allowed to party. Paul Oliver, in his book *The Story of The Blues*, writes:

'Saturday night was for the good times, with the liquor flowing, the shouts and laughter of dancers rising above the noise of a juke band or gin mill piano and sometimes the staccato report of a revolver fired in jest – or in earnest.'

In the North, negroes weren't allowed in speakeasies, so they made their own entertainment. In *Hard Times* by Studs Terkel, Red Saunders, a jazz musician, describes the 'rent' parties.

'You had to have these rent parties during prohibition because there were no night clubs to speak of. They were black speakeasies . . . houses where people lived, with a piano in the front room where people danced. And moonshine, 25c a half pint. Pulverised alcohol, no admission. The money came from the sale of moonshine and supper. Spaghetti and chili . . . the house'd be packed all kinds of way. Six, five, sometimes four rooms, a hundred eighty people would be in it. They were giving a party to get their rent together.'

When electrically amplified automatic phonographs began appearing in the late 1920s, these two types of black locations were the first to welcome them. Here, at last was a vehicle for their own recorded music in their own places. Meyer Parkoff, an operator at the time, recalls that before repeal, Harlem was the main area on the East Coast for the juke box.

'Rather than hiring a band, they would ask me for a phonograph which I would put in on the Saturday and take out after the weekend. This gave them an additional source of income which helped pay the rent, because they didn't have to pay the band, and they made some money from the juke box. There was a lot of that in those days.'

The juke box had arrived. Within ten years it would become one of the dominant themes in American life. At this point it is worth turning our attention to the small group of businessmen who must be given the credit for perceiving the product and creating the industry. Of the five great manufacturing corporations that emerged in the 1930s. J. P. Seeburg was one of the first in the field.

*Early radios like this 'Aeriola Junior' appealed to the insider instinct by providing each listener with his own set of earphones. But speakers quickly came along to make radios the chief source of living-room entertainment in the 1920s.*

# NOTICE!
## STOP

### Help Save The Youth of America
### DON'T BUY NEGRO RECORDS

(If you don't want to serve negroes in your place of business, then do not have negro records on your juke box or listen to negro records on the radio.)

The screaming, idiotic words, and savage music of these records are undermining the morals of our white youth in America.

Call the advertisers of the radio stations that play this type of music and complain to them!

### Don't Let Your Children Buy, or Listen
### To These Negro Records

*Segregationalists are alarmed by the popularity of the blues. (Courtesy Paul Oliver)*

*Mamie Smith and Her Jazz Hounds recording 'Sax-o-phoney Blues' at the Okeh laboratories in New York. (Talking Machine World, 15 November, 1921)*

*To a limited extent, juke boxes and gramophones replaced blues musicians for dancing at juke-joints like Moore's at Yazoo City. (Courtesy Paul Oliver)*

# CHAPTER 5

## Seeburg

JUSTUS P. SEEBURG (Sjoberg) was born in Sweden in 1871 and received his education at the Chalmers Technical Institute in Gothenberg. His father had been a prosperous merchant before he fell on hard times. In 1886, when Justus was sixteen, the family was broke and he decided to leave Sweden to seek his fortune in the New World. He was inclined towards the field of engineering and, on his arrival in America, made straight for Chicago. His first job was with the Markette Piano Company and whether through choice or circumstance, he remained in the musical instrument business throughout his career. He moved on to a better job at the C. S. Smith Piano Factory and thence to the Cable Piano Company, where he held the position of superintendent for several years.

Having served his apprenticeship, he ventured into the operating business, installing electric coin-operated pianos in choice locations in Chicago. This was a profitable business but Seeberg was a production man by temperament and was more interested in making pianos than in operating them.

In 1907, with capital of his own, he established the J. P. Seeburg Piano Company, and manufactured coin-operated electric pianos. He wholeheartedly believed in his product. In the Seeburg catalogue of 1917 he describes the contribution of automatic instruments to society in the following way:

'We live in a remarkable age . . . Today . . . revolutionary inventions are common practice in our everyday life bringing profits, comforts, safety, efficiency, convenience, pleasure and recreation to millions of people every hour and forming the basis of great industries giving employment to millions of persons and using thousands of millions of capital.'

In those days, Seeburg was an aggressive promotor. In a bulletin to his dealers, he wrote,

'You can offer this piano *free* to any Cafe, Lunch Room, Confectionery, Billiard Parlour, Clubroom, Dance Pavilion or Road House. Get *four times* its cost and secure a valid sales contract. Where is the sales resistance to such an offer? That's what makes for sure deal and positive profits in selling and operating *Seeburg*

*Automatic Pianos* and *Orchestrions.*'

The 'Orchestrion' was Seeburg's first product. It was a restyled piano that added mechanically played violin, mandolin, flute, snare drum, cymbal, triangle and other percussive effects to the piano music and was powered pneumatically with electrically driven bellows. The cabinets were finished in oak and mahogany and some were decorated with ornamental art glass. Style 'X' – 'The Expression' – a straight piano 'reproducing expression almost human in accomplishment'; Style 'B' was the 'Artistic Automatic'. These two weighed about 900lb each but were mere lightweights compared to the model 'H': eighteen hundred pounds of piano, xylophone, sixty-eight pipes, mandolin attachment, bass and snare drum, cymbal, triangle and simulated sounds of violin, piccolo, flute and clarinet.

Seeburg ran a paternalistic shop. Almost all his employees were Swedish immigrants, some fresh off the boat. Swedish was spoken in the factory and snuff boxes were to be seen next to many pieces of machinery. There was a company newsletter, *The Seeburg Voice*, a baseball league and other social clubs. It was, by all accounts, one big happy family. By 1920, Seeburg was one of the country's leading player-piano makers; he was a married man with one son.

Then, in 1926, the Brunswick 'Panatrope' was introduced. This was the first all-electric home phonograph. Seeburg knew immediately that this was a major technical breakthrough that would affect the entire automatic music industry. Now, with the much increased range and volume, recorded music could finally be played in locations where, hitherto, its sound would have been drowned out. In 1927, Seeburg discontinued the 'Orchestrion' and began tooling up for an all-electric multi-selection coin-operated disc-playing phonograph.

About 140 miles north-east of Chicago, in Grand Rapids, Michigan, the Automatic Musical Instrument Company had been working on Seeburg's same assumptions since as early as 1925.

The National Piano Manufacturing Company, founded in 1909, manufactured a player-piano

*A Seeburg 'Audiophone' of 1928 (front view of eight-selection mechanism).*

with a selection mechanism. It was an unusual organisation in as much as all the equipment manufactured was sold to and operated by the National Automatic Music Company which was part of National Piano. In this respect, it resembled the structure that Lippincott created in 1888. The fact that National Piano got wind of the changes that were taking place so early, was probably due to their proximity, as operators, to the market. They knew that electric amplification would soon reinstate the phonograph in the better locations; and so they acted accordingly. The two companies were merged in 1925 as a division of Automatic Musical Instrument Company (AMI). At about this time, an inventor, B. C. Kenyon, brought a record changer to Clifford H. Breame, chief engineer at AMI. It was an extremely practical and very advanced record-changing mechanism that would serve the companies' equipment, with

occasional modifications, for almost thirty years. Production began in 1926 and by the end of the following year, 8500 of the new instruments had been placed in locations.

The great Mills Novelty Company had also seen the writing on the wall (see chapter 13) and thus by 1927, three major player-piano manufacturers had moved away from the music box concept and into automatic phonographs. After an absence of twenty years, the phonograph was returning to the old locations.

However, the real architect of the juke box industry was not to be found in the industrial centres of Chicago or New York, or even Grand Rapids. It is to Southern Indiana that we must now travel to discover the vital link between early juke box developments in the 1920s and the major industry that it became in the late 1930s.

*Flappers and their escorts dancing to a juke box in the late 1920s.* (Talking Machine World, *February 1929*)

# CHAPTER 6

## Capehart

HOMER E. CAPEHART says, without a trace of modesty, 'I was the daddy of them all.' Capehart was not an empire builder, but he was a driving force in the industry during its early years. He established a system of merchandising which was adopted by other manufacturers, and it was his system which gave the juke box business its growth, stability and longevity.

Born in 1897, the son of a poor farmer in southern Indiana, he served in the Army during the First World War and upon receiving his discharge he went to work for the J. I. Case Plough Company. He joined the Holcomb & Hoke Manufacturing Company as a salesman in 1921. This company had for many years been manufacturing a line of coin-operated vending machines such as ball-gum dispensers and Butterkist popcorn machines. They were a successful outfit, and Capehart learned a great deal from Holcomb's enthusiastic brand of salesmanship. It was in 1926 that Holcomb & Hoke began manufacturing the 'Electromuse', an automatic phonograph mounted in a square cabinet with a window at the front. This apparatus offered multiple selections and was probably the first of its kind.

By this time, Capehart had risen through the ranks to become sales manager, a key figure in the organisation. Holcomb, who until then had been the company's chief salesman, may have felt threatened by the young Capehart. Capehart was clearly fascinated by the new musical device and was alert to its possibilities. He began to wonder if it might not be possible to play recorded music continuously without having to get up to change the records. He was sure that Americans would respond to such a labour-saving device.

In 1927, while on a sales mission for Holcomb & Hoke in Cleveland, he noticed an article in a newspaper concerning a local man who had invented a device which changed phonograph records for play automatically. To amuse the local readership the article described it as 'the mouse-

*Homer E. Capehart, young businessman.*
(News-Sentinel, *Fort Wayne*)

trap'. Capehart, for one, was not laughing. He lost no time in locating the man, Thomas Small, in his workshop. He asked to see the mechanism work and Small complied. Capehart watched and listened as the stack of records played over and over. Capehart was satisfied that it worked. It was to his mind a substantial improvement on the 'Electromuse' mechanism, and he was not about to stand in the way of progress. He bought it for $500 plus royalties and returned to Indiana with Small and the mouse-trap in tow.

The intentions of the young Capehart at this point in time are not impossible to discern, but the manner in which he conducted himself is most revealing. Professor William Pickett, in his excellent account of Capehart's early career, has written that Capehart 'invited Holcomb to go to a downtown Indianapolis hotel to meet Small and see the fancy record changer. Capehart recalled later that Holcomb watched it work with a certain ill-concealed fascination.' If Capehart really believed that Holcomb would embrace him and offer him a directorship, he was sadly mistaken. Holcomb, although an excellent salesman, was obstinate and may have felt that he was about to be upstaged by Capehart. Pickett relates that Holcomb 'abruptly asked Small what he proposed to do with it'. Small replied, 'Ask Mr Capehart, I sold it to him'. Holcomb turned, muttered words to the effect that he was just a thirty-year-old kid who worked for his company, and stomped out. The next morning, Holcomb had L. D. Thomas, the company's general manager and treasurer, tell Capehart he was fired.

Capehart held all the trumps. He was young, arrogant, decisive, owned a promising invention and retained the loyalty of a dozen top Holcomb & Hoke men who were soon to join him, including, ironically, L. D. Thomas. All he needed now was money, and in 1927 there was plenty about. Through Homer McKee, who did Holcomb & Hoke's advertising, Capehart made the acquaintance of three Indiana businessmen in the automobile trade. They put up $10,000 for the purpose of developing the Small mechanism to production. Work was progressing well in the Indianapolis workshop when Ralph C. Lockwood, an attorney whom Capehart had hired, reported a number of possible patent infringements in Small's invention. Since Capehart had purchased the device without doing a patent search, the car dealers became jumpy and urged Capehart to drop the whole idea. Undeterred, he countered by buying them out with a $5000 promissory note payable in six months and immediately began looking for new finance.

He found it in the somewhat more substantial persons of J. W. Caswell and Winfred Runyan, owners of a large furniture factory in Huntington, Indiana. He persuaded them that automatic phonographs were the thing; furthermore, he would, with their help, be in a position to place large orders with them for Caswell-Runyan cabinets to house the record changer. The Capehart Automatic Phonograph Corporation was thus formed. Caswell and Runyan bought $50,000 worth of stock in the company and gave Capehart an office in a small five-room bungalow adjacent to the plant until such time as he could move into larger premises.

Capehart's firm began manufacturing the 'Orchestrope' in the spring of 1928. It was the first automatic record player that could play both sides of its capacity of twenty-eight records. Enclosed in a fine wood cabinet it was also supplied with remote-control wall-boxes for use in restaurants. Capehart's objective had been to build a machine that was superior to the 'Electromuse'. The 'Orchestrope' was well made, had a

*Capehart's first office in Huntington, Indiana.* (News-Sentinel, *Fort Wayne*)

*Capehart's factory during the Caswell-Runyan period.* (News-Sentinel, *Fort Wayne*)

*The new plant at Fort Wayne, Indiana.* (News-Sentinel, *Fort Wayne*)

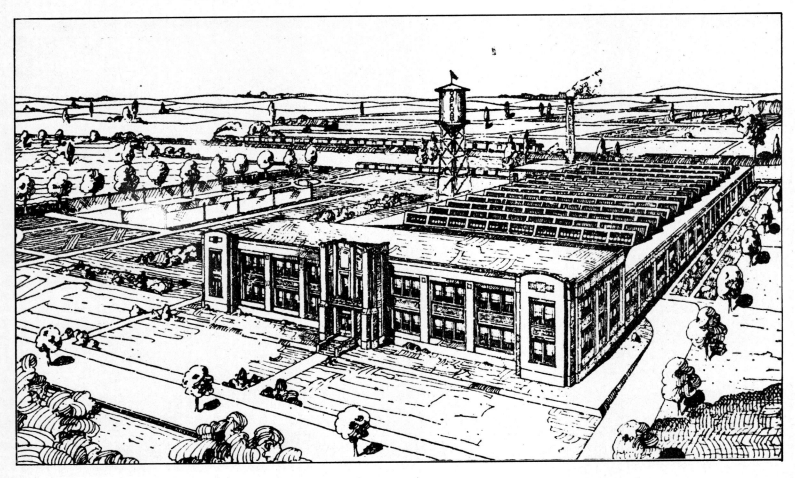

resonant tone, was versatile and handsome in appearance. It was more in the class of Victor's 'Borgia II' radio phonograph which had retailed at $1000.

The 'Orchestrope' was shown at the Detroit Aviation Show and later in October at the Chicago Radio Show where the acclaim it received was second only to that of 'television' which was given its first public showing at the same time. By July, six hundred and twenty-five machines had been sold at $785.50 apiece.

Capehart's greatest stroke at this stage was not in production, but in merchandising. Using techniques he had learned from Holcomb, he established a network of dealers throughout the country who would display, promote and sell Capehart equipment to independent operators. It was the introduction of this middleman which would help the industry to develop in the way that it did.

As the balmy days of the unusually hot summer wore on, and the wheels of Homer E. Capehart's little factory rhythmically turned, disaster struck. Reports began arriving from bemused dealers that the records that were stacked on a central shaft and held in position from the middle by screws were warping in the summer heat. As the stack would lower itself, the records were getting crushed (as only shellac can). Suddenly, Capehart's 'Orchestrope' had become, to quote Pickett, 'the Capehart record eater'.

Instantly, Capehart sent out telegrams to all his dealers, reassuring them that the fault was minor and that the company would take back every defective machine, repair it and return it at no cost to the dealer whatsoever. In point of fact, the fault was anything but minor. Capehart's talented engineer Edward E. Collison – late of Holcomb & Hoke – had not done his homework. He now set about redesigning the system. To make matters worse, it was at this time that Caswell, Runyan and Capehart all received identical letters from the Victor Talking Machine Company advising them that the 'Orchestrope' was in breach of a number of patents and that action would follow.

Yet the combined effect of six hundred and twenty-five 'Orchestropes' sitting idle in the Huntington factory waiting for the harrassed Collison to work out a solution, plus the spectre of the giant Victor Company of New Jersey breathing fiery smoke over the diminutive Indiana enterprise in no wit ruffled the irrepressible Capehart. It was, however, more than the elder partners could bear; Caswell and Runyan wanted out.

Under some pressure at this point, Capehart was able to study the problem with perfect clarity. He needed three things: a new backer, a new mechanism and for Victor to disappear. Naturally he got all three.

After some research, he located the ideal punter; Charles Neizer, director of the Tri-state Loan Company of Fort Wayne, Indiana. To this otherwise conservative banker Capehart explained that things were not as bad as they might at first appear. Had he not successfully sold over six hundred 'Orchestropes' at four times their manufacturing cost, thereby grossing just under $500,000 in less than four months of production? Were it not for a small irritant, the equipment would still be in location earning thousands of dollars, and orders would be pouring in for more machines. Then Capehart produced the carrot; he would move his whole operation to Fort Wayne, thereby providing jobs for the townsfolk and a stimulus for local industry. Neizer signed.

Tri-state Loans bought $200,000 of preferred stock in the Capehart Automatic Phonograph Corporation, Neizer became chairman, and the name of the company was shortened to the Capehart Corporation. At the time, the total value of Capehart's corporate assets was listed as $278,000. The arrangement went into effect on 27 May 1929 and while the factory was being built to his specifications, Capehart flew to Pittsburg and for $25,000 bought a new record changer that allowed the records to lie flat, one on top of the other. Collison installed the new mechanism and within six months, the 'Orchestropes' began to return to their original locations.

In the promotional literature, Capehart had assured the operators that,

'Capehart instruments are sold exclusively through carefully selected dealers. The entire Capehart organisation is behind your Capehart dealer in its effort to make you another enthusiastic Capehart user. Most certainly, you may buy with confidence.'

He had kept faith with his customers and so his reputation grew. The Victor Talking Machine Company had been taken over by the Radio Corporation of America and was undergoing complete reorganisation – so there was no more trouble from that quarter. On 13 June 1929 the new factory at Fort Wayne was officially opened. This was a great triumph. After three days of partying, which Pickett describes as 'an occasion . . . unsurpassed by Capehart extravaganzas until the Wurlitzer Century Club Convention eight years later', production began in earnest. Three hundred workers were turning out twenty-five instruments per day. A Capehart 'Orchestrope' was located inside the factory sending out recorded music to the workers on the shop floor and, through a system of outside speakers, to passers-by. The company newsletter reported in October 1929 that 'every afternoon and evening, large numbers of cars parked in front of Capehart's "Singing Tower" to listen to the splendid programmes offered.'

Capehart's was one of the first factories in America to have a group medical, casualty and life insurance plan. He took a personal interest in all areas of production and knew most of his workers by name. In the words of Pickett,

'The money poured in. Despite the increased price for the model "Orchestropes" (from $785.50 to $1250), they continued to sell. A Des Moins, Iowa, dealer wrote Capehart in 1929 that one of his buyers, a local sweet shop prioprietor, had

*Capehart stand at the Los Angeles Radio Show, 1-7 September, 1929.*

*Edward Collison, Capehart's chief engineer. (News-Sentinel, Fort Wayne)*

*Menu for the dinner to celebrate the opening of the Fort Wayne factory on 13 June, 1929.*

## Menu

**The Musical Marvel of the Age**
*Boston Clam Chowder*

**Electric Pick-up**   **Maximum Consumption**   **Rejector Buttons**
*Hearts of Celery*        *Garden Radishes*            *Olives*

**The Club Model—56 Selections**
*Minute Steak—Fresh Mushrooms*

**The Aristocrat**                      **Musical Variety**
*Country Gentleman Corn*              *French Fried Potatoes*

**Capehart Chassis—Record-Changing Mechanism**
*Head Lettuce—Thousand Island Dressing*

**3rd Stage of Amplification**        **Finished Installation**
*Strawberry Ice Cream*                      *Cake*

**To be played on both sides**   **Amplified Volume Controlled**
*Rolls*                                      *Coffee or Tea*

receipts of no less than $28 per week from one "Orchestrope".'

By the autumn of 1929, the Capehart Corporation was doing the equivalent of an annual business of $4 million with a range of seven machines. Every operating possibility was being explored from the 'Club' model (without coin-slot) for plush halls, to the 'Park' model (fully weather-proofed) for use outdoors.

And then in October the New York Stock Market collapsed and, during the next few years, many otherwise balanced American executives would be falling out of tall buildings. Not Homer E. Capehart. In November, during an interview with a Fort Wayne reporter, he expressed his optimism and announced plans to increase output to $12,000,000 in 1930. The following year, after having to lay off some workers,

his enthusiasm had not deserted him. 'What business needs,' he said, 'is a stimulus. Confidence is something that has been lacking in the last ten months but is now apparent everywhere.'

Characteristically, Capehart put his money where his mouth was. On 10 October 1930 he ordered the production of 500 record changers per week and announced plans to increase output to 40,000 per annum. At the end of this year, he did admit the presence of some unsettling factors in the economy and referred vaguely to 'the depression we have just passed through'.

The recent business decline of the summer of 1930 he relegated to the 'normal operation of the business cycle. There is no question in my mind,' he went on, 'but that the business depression hit rock bottom during the first two weeks of August'. Clearly, the man was a positive thinker.

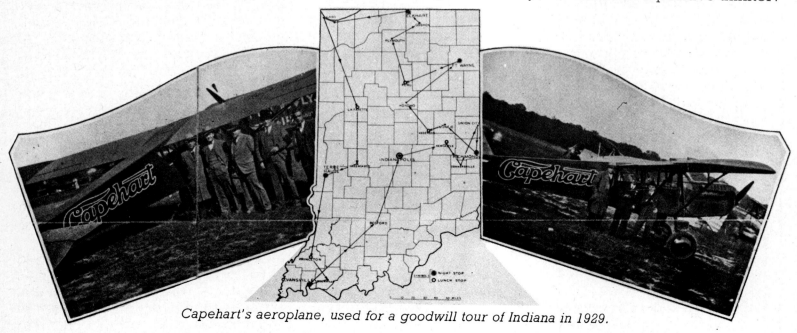

*Capehart's aeroplane, used for a goodwill tour of Indiana in 1929.*

Ironically, Capehart was probably right. If all American businessmen had had his confidence and daring, recovery would have come much sooner and perhaps might have been achieved without the help of the New Deal. It is at least arguable that Capehart himself could have survived the Depression and emerged as the leading juke box manufacturer in the country.

But Capehart made one fatal and almost unforgivable error. Some time near the end of 1929, he decided to stop manufacturing the coin-operated range and concentrate on home phonographs. One can only speculate as to his motives. He doubtless received encouraging reports from his dealers on the response of the public to the home models. His acute business instinct may have told him that phonographs were coming back. There was perhaps an even more important motive. Ever since his days at Holcomb & Hoke, Capehart had been preoccupied with quality. He was, in his way, a perfectionist, and had it in the back of his mind to manufacture the world's finest automatic phonograph one day. Early in 1930, he purchased a record changer from the Columbia Phonograph Company. It was a Ralph Erbe design which did much the same as the 'Orchestrope' mechanism but with more efficiency and in half the space. It was built into a cabinet made from the finest walnut; with the very latest electrical equipment, it had, according to Capehart, the highest fidelity in the world. It was the definitive phonograph, the last word in luxury. Known as the Capehart 400 or, more simply, the 'Capehart', it retailed at $1095. It was one of eleven home phonographs in the range.

He used every trick he knew in his determination to make the 'Capehart' a success. In March 1930, the company embarked upon a national advertising campaign in the *Saturday Evening Post* and in *House and Garden*. Capehart personally briefed his salesmen and extended credit to the dealers to cover the costs of a new shipment of phonographs. He supplied his dealers with lists of persons in their area whose net worth was $50,000 plus. Capehart's enthusiasm and hard work payed important dividends. A list of his customers reads like a guest list for one of Mrs Vanderbilt's parties: Andrew Citreon, Alfred P. Sloan, George B. Warner, the King of Siam,

Vincent Astor, Carl G. Fisher, R. J. Reynolds, Florenz Ziegfield, John Wanamaker Jr, the Sultan of Morocco, Clara Bow and Raymond Navarro. The name Capehart was uttered in the same breath as Steinway or Wurlitzer. His pride is particularly evident in a story he enjoyed telling about how, in 1946, as a United States Senator he was visiting London as part of a top-level American delegation. While having drinks in the Members' Club at the House of Commons, Lady Astor (herself an American) called across to Capehart, 'Senator, won't you let me have a Capehart?' 'Why, yes, madame,' he called back, 'I believe every pretty lady should have a little Capehart.'

Capehart had achieved his goal but he had been a little impatient; if he had continued with his plebian juke boxes, he would have surely been on Mrs Vanderbilt's list himself. But in 1930, Capehart was 33 years old, married with three children and living in great luxury. He was Indiana's own boy wonder and felt that he was ready for greater things. As his later career would show, his desire for prestige and status was greater than his ambition for financial power.

No one was worse hit by the Depression than the phonograph industry. As we saw in chapter five, America's rejection of the phonograph was decisive. Capehart's sales dropped through 1931, and many of his dealers defaulted. Awareness of his mistake may have dawned at about this time, but he no longer had the capital with which to change course. He now perceived that if there was a market for phonographs in an America with thirteen million unemployed, it must be cheap, and it must be coin-operated.

In February 1932, Capehart was fired as president and general manager of the Capehart Corporation. 'Neizer sort of went crazy', he later recalled. Now he was almost broke; he had lost the rights to all Capehart patents and the prospect of raising new finance in 1932 must have seemed remote indeed. Despite his failure, he had shown himself to be a businessman of exceptional talent and motivation. Even now, his optimism was undiminished and if his self-confidence had suffered a serious blow, he didn't let it show. He began looking for a new opening and when one presented itself in the Wurlitzer organisation, he grabbed it with both hands.

*The 'Capehart' was a luxury item that was displayed only in the swankiest stores.*

# CHAPTER 7

## Wurlitzer

THE INVOLVEMENT of the Wurlitzer family with musical instruments dates back to 1659. Nicholas Wurlitzer of Schilback, Saxony, was a lute-maker, as were his son and his grandson after him. Of the following generation of Wurlitzers, Christian Gottfried, born in 1807, was either smarter than his forebears or no good with his hands, because he was the family's first businessman. He established a small concern in Schoeneck (near Schilback) buying and selling musical instruments and brought up his son, Franz Rudolph, to take over the business.

Rudolph had plans of his own, however, and in 1853 left his native Saxony and sailed to the United States. He landed penniless at Hoboken, New Jersey, and moved around the country, like thousands of others, looking for work and somewhere to settle down. His first job was in a grocery store, then as a porter in a dry goods factory. After a spell as a door-to-door salesman he even tried his hand at banking with the firm of Heidel-back and Seasongood in Cincinnati.

It was commonplace at that time for the European immigrants to live by the skills and crafts that they had acquired in their old countries. Whether or not this was Rudolph's intention, he was too much a Wurlitzer to ignore the fact that the standard of craftsmanship in American musical instruments could not hold a light to that of Saxony. He saved $700 and sent it back to Schoeneck with a list of instruments he wanted to sell in Cincinnati plus detailed shipping instructions. In this manner, he built up a prosperous import business and established a reputation for his commercial abilities. On the eve of the Civil War, he was awarded a Government contract to supply drums and bugles to the Union forces and by the end of the war he had become the largest band-instrument maker in the United States. In 1865 he diversified still further by establishing the first of a chain of retail outlets in Chicago. In 1880 Rudolph, by now joined by his younger brother Anton,

*Left: 'With 100,000 soda fountains . . . 200,000 diner cars, lunchrooms and restaurants in the United States . . . the field for Wurlitzer counter models is in the same undeveloped stage as was the console model field five years ago' – Wurlitzer publicity to operators in 1940. (Courtesy M. Trussell)*

*Right: Counter model 41, 1940. 2010 shipped. (Courtesy M. Trussell)*

went into the manufacturing of pianos.

Wurlitzer became interested in the field of coin-operation at the start of the nickel-and-slot phonograph boom and in 1893 became distributor for the Regina Music Box Company of New Jersey, late of Germany; this association lasted until 1903 when Wurlitzer decided to move over to phonographs. Wurlitzer became a principal dealer for the products of the Victor Talking Machine Company; this relationship was cemented by close personal ties and endured into the 1950s.

In 1908, the Wurlitzer Company acquired the plant and business of another old friend of the family, de Kleist, who manufactured carnival equipment and organs at his factory in North Tonowanda, near Buffalo in New York State. With the advent of moving pictures, the company became famous for the pipe organ known as the 'Wurlitzer Motion Picture Orchestra'. By 1910, a newer model of this organ, the 'Mighty Wurlitzer', began to accompany the antics of silent movie idols. It was this machine that firmly imprinted the family name in the minds of a generation. To the public, Wurlitzer meant organs. In banking circles, Wurlitzer was synonymous with reliability. In 1909, the company assets were valued at $1,000,000; by 1921, they had grown to $6,000,000. Rudolph Wurlitzer, the founder of the business, died in 1914, leaving his three sons to run the business. The youngest, Farny, was put in charge of the manufacturing division at North Tonawanda.

In the late 1920s, the motion picture industry began talking and the market for the 'Mighty Wurlitzer' contracted sharply. In addition, there was a slackening in demand for its piano products. Although production at North Tonawanda had been drastically reduced, Wurlitzer was able to absorb the setback. By 1928, however, the company was in difficulties, due to an acute lack of liquidity from assets tied up in real estate, mainly Wurlitzer retail outlets throughout the United States. When the crash came in November 1929, Wurlitzer was caught off-balance. The company's stock fell from a high of $119 per share in 1928 to $10 by 1932. The company, $5 million in debt, had to begin selling refrigerators and furniture in its search for profitable products.

Meanwhile, the indefatigable Capehart had moved into a new factory in Fort Wayne. He was restrained from using his own name for his products and so he took the name of Packard, the small piano company he had bought out (which happened, conveniently, to be a near anagram of Capehart). In November 1932, the Packard Manufacturing Company was incorporated.

The loss of his business had had a sobering effect on Capehart. He didn't have to pretend any longer that economic recovery was just around the corner, and he knew that he would never be able to raise finance in Indiana since his debacle with Charles Neizer. He braced himself for a long hard slog. Although he still had his eyes

*Left: Counter model 71, 1940. 4506 shipped.*

*Right: Wurlitzer promotional material for the operator.*
(*Courtesy M. Trussell*)

Check These
# WURLITZER
## COUNTER MODEL
*Locations In Your Locality*

ROADSIDE STANDS

AIR TERMINALS

GENERAL STORES

FILLING STATIONS

ICE CREAM STORES

PUBLIC SWIMMING POOLS

FOUNTAIN-LUNCHEONETTES

CONFECTIONERY STORES

INDUSTRIAL RESTAURANTS

DINERS

TAVERNS

CIGAR STORES

POOL ROOMS

YMCA's—YWCA's

LODGE ROOMS

SOCIAL CLUBS

BEAUTY SHOPPES

SUMMER RESORTS

BARBER SHOPS

COCKTAIL LOUNGES

BOWLING ALLEYS

DRUG STORES

BARBECUE STANDS

RESTAURANTS

TEA ROOMS

COFFEE SHOPS

HOTELS

DELICATESSEN STORES

EXCURSION BOATS

BUS TERMINALS

INDUSTRIAL RECREATION ROOMS

MILK BARS

*YOUR LOCALITY*

LUNCH ROOMS

TOURIST CAMPS

AMUSEMENT PARKS

GOLF and BOATING CLUBS

● Right in your locality there are hundreds of locations where a Wurlitzer Counter Model will pay big profits.

Put a Wurlitzer Counter Model in every one.

Don't wait until the field is crowded. Write, wire or phone for prices now!—and boost your income to new high levels this summer.

The Rudolph Wurlitzer Company, North Tonawanda, New York. Canadian Factory: RCA-Victor Co. Ltd., Montreal, Quebec, Canada.

**A NAME FAMOUS IN MUSIC FOR OVER TWO HUNDRED YEARS**

firmly set upon automatic phonographs, he was, for the time being, looking for a product that was cheaper to produce and which would sell during a depression. Lammerd and Mitchell, two Capehart engineers who had been released by the new management, had joined their former boss at Packard. They had been working on a record player and Capehart thought that he might be able to sell it to someone in the phonograph business; he guessed (correctly) that there would be a market for a cheap record player.

In February 1933, Capehart embarked on a sales mission that would take him across the country. His first stop was the Wurlitzer factory at North Tonawanda. He had heard that they were making a radio called the 'Mohawk' that was suitable for plugging into record players, and thought that he might now persuade them to buy a record player.

Capehart arrived early in the day and found himself passed aimlessly from one purchasing agent to another. Only after complaining about such treatment did he meet Farny R. Wurlitzer, who had heard of the famous 'Capehart' phonograph and graciously called Capehart in.

Farny saw before him a young man with a shock of red hair who looked like a middleweight boxer at the end of his career. Capehart, at his best when he was selling, proceeded to give Farny the old routine, and to his credit, succeeded in selling Farny a few of his record players. But Mr Wurlitzer seemed more interested in hearing about Capehart's Fort Wayne corporation and its noted product; Capehart realised that it wasn't a record player that Farny was looking for, but an automatic phonograph.

Capehart rapidly took stock of the situation. Wurlitzer had obviously heard about the success of the new 'juke boxes' and was beginning to wonder whether this might not be a good product for his company. In an instant, Capehart saw an opportunity, and he grabbed it with both hands. He proceeded to sell Farny on the idea of making juke boxes and at the same time left him in no doubt that what Homer E. Capehart didn't know about automatic phonographs wasn't worth knowing.

So confident was he of the impression he had made, that he immediately headed for Chicago where he knew of a first-class phonograph mechanism which was up for sale. A small manufacturing concern called Simplex had developed a multi-selection mechanism, invented by a Mr Erickson. The company had designed a cabinet and had even manufactured ten of these 'Debutantes' before they found themselves in financial difficulties.

Capehart, relying on his reputation in the phonograph business, signed a contract with them in late March 1933 which stated that he was either to buy the multi-selector and all the remaining assets of Simplex for $50,000, within six months, or sell the 'Simplex' for Erickson.

When Capehart returned to Fort Wayne, there was a letter waiting for him from Wurlitzer, which

asked him if he knew of a coin-operated phonograph which Wurlitzer might buy and produce at North Tonawanda.

Replied Capehart on 3 April 1933:

'On my return to the office, I find your letter in regard to a coin-operated phonograph.

'I have just what you need to manufacture in your plant – the best selective coin automatic phonograph I have ever seen. . .

'I have taken over the sale of this business and would operate it myself if I had the funds.

'With the return of beer and good times, you should sell 25,000 units in the next three years – and make a long profit. . .

'I would like to run up to North Tonawanda the latter part of this week and talk the matter over with you in detail.'

Capehart knew that the 'Simplex' was as good as sold, but he was looking for something more. He understood that Wurlitzer, with their enormous plant, their expertise and financial backing, were in a position to develop the automatic phonograph to its full potential. Quite naturally, Capehart would not settle for just a profit – he wanted some of the action.

Farny had made his own calculations before composing that fateful letter to Capehart. Not only was he convinced that Wurlitzer should be selling automatic phonographs, but also that they had not a moment to lose. He was well enough informed to know that the repeal of Prohibition was imminent and that a huge market for musical entertainment would open up. He needed someone with experience and drive to set the plan in motion.

Thus the needs and aspirations of these two very different men dovetailed to perfection. Whether or not Farny Wurlitzer realized that, in the spring of 1935, Capehart had no money, no business and was driving a Ford, he gave him a generous deal. Wurlitzer paid Capehart $57,000 for Simplex. He would receive 22,000 shares of Wurlitzer stock if sales reached a certain value and he would be Vice-President and General Sales Manager of Wurlitzer (Tonawanda Division); his salary was to be linked to turnover (in 1937 he was earning $68,000). Capehart's dogged determination and unflagging optimism had finally paid off.

He arrived at North Tonawanda in June 1933. He brought with him eight of his old regional and district managers and his trusted assistant James E. Broyles. He moved his family into a large home in one of Buffalo's exclusive suburbs and then, with characteristic energy, set about organising the conversion of the plant to coin-operated phonograph production.

Throughout his years with Wurlitzer, Capehart was given a free hand to run the phonograph business. Farny may not have approved of the way he chewed cigars, but he liked the way he did business. The Wurlitzer records depict Farny as being much loved by his workers, each of whom 'he knew by name'. It is unlikely that this was the case; Farny's responsibilities were in his capacity as financier during this period. But still he

*Left: Counter model 61, late 1930s, early 1940s. 8260 shipped.*

*Below left: Model 35, manufactured in 1936. 99 shipped.*

*Below right: Model 416, 1937. 1003 shipped.*

found time to tend to the roses which were his pride and joy.

In 1934, AMI, Seeburg and Mills were turning out automatic phonographs as fast as they could make them. Their total output for that year was in the region of fifteen thousand and they must have thought that, all things considered, they were doing pretty well. That was before Wurlitzer arrived. Capehart had promised Farny 25,000 juke boxes before the end of 1936; in fact they shipped 63,000.

The first year had been spent in tooling up and in laying the foundations for a nationwide network of dealers. Forty territories were allocated, district managers were given lectures and booklets explaining how 'Cape' wanted things done. Servicemen from all over the country came to North Tonawanda to receive training for the 'Simplex'. Capehart was at his most affable in these new circumstances. With the onerous responsibility of ownership now removed, he was able to concentrate all his creative energy into organisation and promotion. He chose the very best people for his distributors. Established businessmen were attracted to the 'coin-op' industry perhaps for the first time because Wurlitzer was involved. Banks were prepared to extend credit to anyone associated with Wurlitzer.

In 1934, Capehart set the dials to about sixty phonographs per week while the organisation was being put through its paces. In 1935, output was increased to 300 per week and in 1936, 900 per week, putting the total output that year at 44,397. 1936 was a turning point for the Wurlitzer company. For the first time in seven years, they went into the black with a net profit of $550,000. By the end of this year, the assets had risen from $13m to $20m. In October 1937, they shipped $2,000,000 worth of phonographs and in November 1937 holders of preferred Wurlitzer stock collected back dividends of $40.25 per share.

Capehart was watching events at the end of 1937. Although the company had shipped over 40,000 juke boxes in that year, sales were down 5% on the previous year, and this was happening to all the manufacturers. The period of rapid expansion had, it appeared, come to an end. In the fall of the previous year Wurlitzer very nearly had a one million dollar surplus of unsold phonographs. But Capehart had seen the danger and had embarked on a tour of the largest cities in the United States giving a sales convention at each stop. The finale was held at the Waldorf Astoria where he gave a lavish party for operators of the New York area.

His district managers were sending him regular reports about what was happening on the ground. Every possible juke box location was now occupied. Some fifty per cent of them contained Wurlitzer equipment, a total of 105,000 phonographs. The operators reckoned that they could get a good six years use out of a machine before it was ready for scrapping. The annual sales to these operators would, at this rate, stabilise at 16,000 units, and, in commercial terms, this was

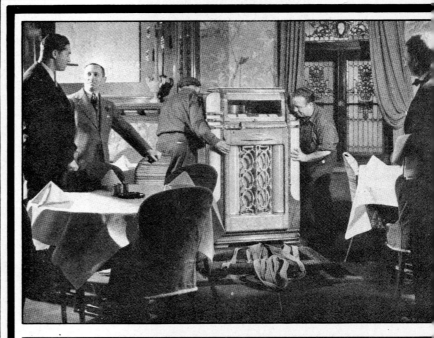

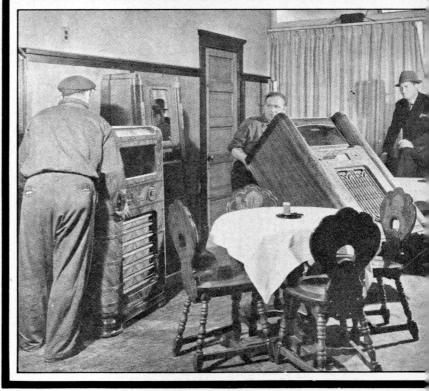

*Metamorphosis of a juke box: it starts out in the top locations and after a rapid social decline ends up as scrap. Manufacturers encouraged operators to trade in their old juke boxes long before their useful life was actually over. The earlier machines were then broken up; this practice was responsible for the near-extinction of many models. Note the operator, who is portrayed as a 'big shot' in this cunning piece of Wurlitzer promotional material.*

# SMASHED TO PIECES

*Wurlitzer 616A 1938.*

*'So that's how they work!' Young lady inside a Wurlitzer 616.*

*'A favourite with drug-store patrons'. Wurlitzer promotion for the model 61.*

*'Cape' takes the pledge – to get behind Wurlitzer operators everywhere and make 1938 the biggest year for them in the history of the coin machine industry. It was not honoured.*

*Homer Capehart in rube duds at a Century Club convention.*

not a happy prospect for the manufacturers. Capehart was an aggressive salesman and was determined to hold the line at at least double that figure. He had several possible courses of action.

It was not thought that a reduction in the price of the equipment would achieve the best results. Apart from cutting the profit margin, it might actually be counter-productive if the other manufacturers were to follow suit. Easier credit for the 'ops' was also ruled out at this stage; not only would this increase the risk of default, but it would encourage marginal operators to compete with the established ones, and this again would be counter-productive. Capehart didn't want to make it easier for the operators; he wanted them to work harder.

Capehart announced a curtailment of production and sales by 40% 'regardless of demands made upon us to do otherwise'. This was part of a programme for 'controlled production' in order to 'stabilise the industry'. At the same time, Wurlitzer, like the other manufacturers, was offering generous part-exchange terms to operators with old equipment. Older models, it was explained, would not be allowed to compete against the newer equipment for locations, and to emphasise the point, the company distributed photographs of workmen attacking helpless old juke boxes with sledgehammers. This would have the effect of upgrading the equipment in the secondary locations, therefore providing more revenue for the operator. From the manufacturer's point of view, if the operator was forced to increase his rate of replacement, it would mean a proportionate increase in turnover.

Finally, Capehart made an appeal to his 'ops' to provide a better service to the location owner and accept a lower percentage of the revenue. In this way, they would win all the best locations, make more money and buy more Wurlitzer phonographs.

Capehart's programme does not bear too close an examination. How could he offer generous trade-ins and 'curtail production' at the same time? In point of fact, sales were reduced by only 25% and not 40% as promised and this was probably a reflection of the general business decline of that year. Nevertheless it had a certain logic and Capehart had a lot of charm. He prepared for a second nationwide crusade and in July 1938 hit the road. As Pickett puts it:

'He and his entourage embarked on a 14,500 mile, thirty-day tour of the twenty-one largest cities in the United States. It was a combined cocktail hour, banquet, community sing and floor show for as many as twelve hundred and rarely as few as four hundred Wurlitzer operators in each city . . . Capehart was principal speaker at each banquet and gave his address under a fringed banner on which large white letters said, "Welcome! Uncle Homer." '

Capehart loved parties; in 1936 he had started the Century Club, whose membership was restricted to those operators who had bought over a hundred Wurlitzer phonographs. At the end of

August, the annual conventions were held in the grounds of the plant at North Tonawanda; the twelve hundred members ate steamed clams, drank and sang while Capehart horsed around; he was a very popular man, and he had a way with the girls. He always said that one had to look after the ladies, and made a point of knowing the wives of all his hundreds of business associates by name.

Wurlitzer never again achieved the 1936 output of 44,397 juke boxes. In 1938, output fell to 33,721 and stayed at about the thirty thousand mark up till the War. Capehart had not succeeded in wresting locations from the other manufacturers; Rock-Ola was a strong competitor who had promotional gimmicks of his own. Seeburg were coming out with better equipment every year and AMI and Mills always accounted for a steady share of the market. There was even room for the little man, like Gabel and, later, Filben. However, Wurlitzer were still number one, and even if they weren't quite as dominating as people at that time imagined (estimates ranged from seventy to eighty per cent), they always accounted for at least fifty per cent of the total output of the industry.

Early in 1938, Capehart had begun to get restless at Wurlitzer. According to Professor Pickett,

'In January 1939, he sent a letter to all Wurlitzer customers announcing that Carl E. Johnson, the factory manager, would replace him as manager of the North Tonawanda division, and that M. G. Hammergren of the company's Cincinnati office would take over his duties as general sales manager. Although he remained through 1939 in an advisory capacity at half salary ($32,500), he said he wanted to spend more time in connection with the general administrative problems of our company. But, on 5 January 1940, he announced his resignation as vice-president and remarked that he had completed what he had set out to accomplish at Wurlitzer. He added that he would devote his time to farming "on a big scale in Indiana, oil production, and politics – but maybe you had better not mention politics, I am not a very good politician." His disclaimer hid what in retrospect was fairly clear; he had caught the political fever.'

Pickett also suggests that Farny Wurlitzer was probably glad to see him go. Perhaps he felt that Capehart had made too much money while he was at Wurlitzer. But Capehart had been worth every penny; giving him his job back in 1933 was possibly the best decision Farny ever made. If the Wurlitzer people thought for a moment that their enthusiastic and experienced general sales manager was in any way expendable in 1938, they were sadly wrong, as events ten years later were to show. But Capehart was not a 'company man' and, by 1938, he had perceived that there were no more mountains to climb in the industry.

After he left, he got himself elected to the Senate where he served for a full three terms before retiring to his farms in Indiana. His life-long hero was Abe Lincoln, and Capehart earned a reputation for being an honest politician and a good representative of the people of his home state. I spoke to him late in 1975 at his ranch; and as I was preparing to leave Mr Capehart asked me who I was going to see next.

'Mr Rockola senior,' I replied.

'Is he still alive?'

'Yes.'

'He is, is he? Well, I've got a message I want you to give to him. Tell him that he made good juke boxes, but I had to show him the way. And tell him about my farms. You won't forget, now?'

'Cape' plays softball with the boys at the 1938 Century Club convention.

'Wurlitzer will long remember the bevies of fashionable femininity, the busloads of pulchritude,' says the caption to this 1938 convention picture. The wives were given a special party – Capehart's axiom was to 'look after the ladies'.

**PEOPLE:** (1) "Babe" Kaufman smiles for the birdie. (2) R. C. Rolfing, Farny Wurlitzer, Rudolph Wurlitzer have the time of their lives. (3) Bill Mahle makes "moosic" for the gang. (4) Mr. and Mrs. ? ? ? (5) One gal the boys didn't dare go near. (6) Manny Ehrenfeld, Passaic, shows his wife what pull can do. (7) J. F. Johnson, Omaha old timer, and son. (8) W. H. Milam, Texas old timer, says "How" to a friend from home. (9) E. T. Mape of Frisco with Ernie Petering and Joe Bergeson of Minnesota (10) General Credit Manager "Bill" Bolles and Sid Siegel.

*Happy days are here again. Page from the 1938 convention brochure.*

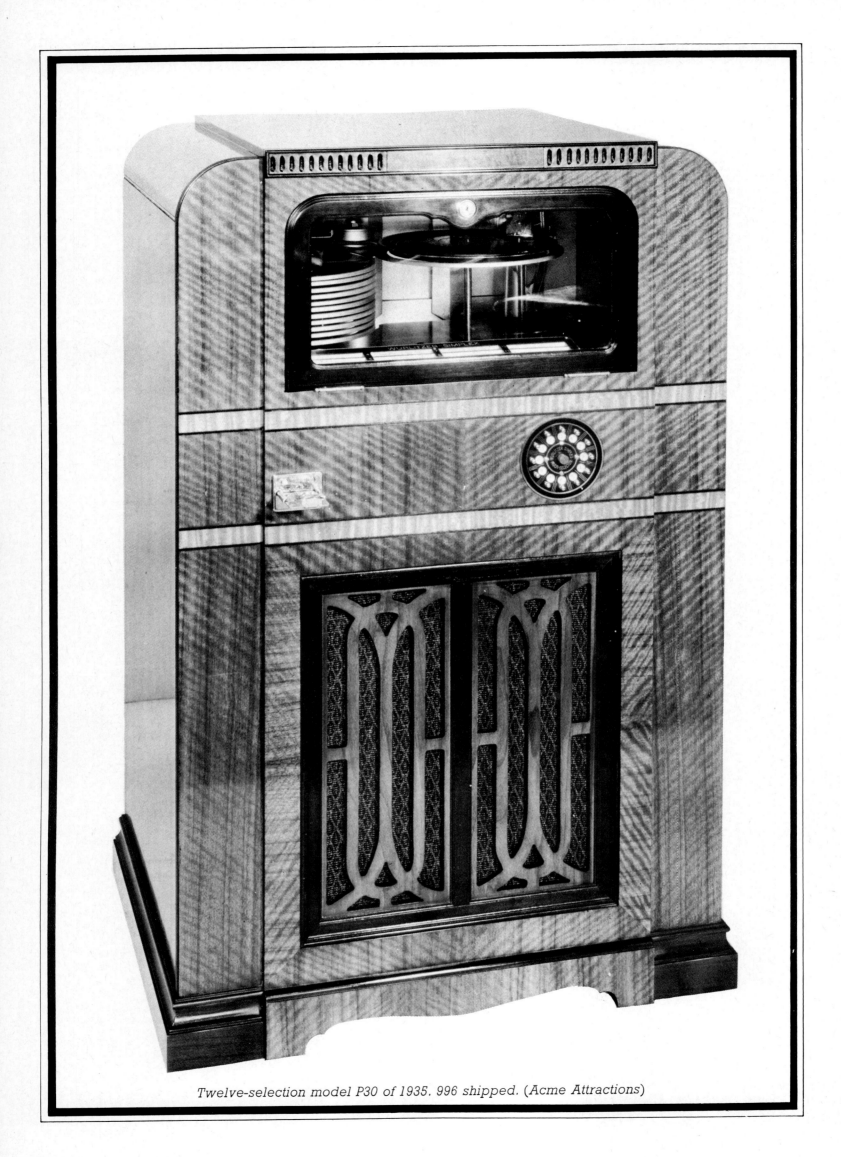

*Twelve-selection model P30 of 1935. 996 shipped. (Acme Attractions)*

*Twenty-four selection model 750 of 1940. 18,387 shipped. (Acme Attractions)*

Top: The North Tonawanda plant in a recent photograph. (Courtesy A. D. Palmer)

Centre: Farny Wurlitzer.

Above: Rudolph Wurlitzer (1831-1914).

Right: Art Leard, Wurlitzer's permanent master of ceremonies.

HEADS UP!

IS EVERYBODY HAPPY?

PUBLISHED BY THE RUDOLPH WURLITZER COMPANY, NORTH TONAWANDA, N. Y., VOL. 1, NO. 3, OCTOBER 1938

WURLITZER CENTURY CLUB
FIRST ANNUAL CONVENTION
•
WIND-UP BANQUET, STATLER HOTEL
GRAND BALL ROOM, AUGUST 27, 1937

*Top:* One thousand of America's toughest operators.

*Centre:* Capehart talking to the 'ops' in New Orleans.

*Above:* Capehart will stop at nothing to make a sale.

*Left:* Cardboard cut-out of Capehart with his district manager, entertaining the Illinois operators at the Hotel Knickerbocker in 1938.

*Model 600, 1938. 9777 shipped. (Courtesy Mike Jordan)*

*Wurlitzer-Simplex 'Modernistic' 316, 1936-7. 8002 shipped.*

*Wurlitzer-Simplex standard model 616, 1937. 23,706 shipped.*

*Wurlitzer-Simplex 'Modernistic' 716, 1937. 2600 shipped.*

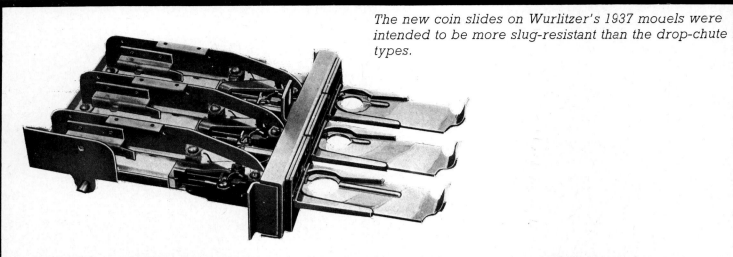

*The new coin slides on Wurlitzer's 1937 models were intended to be more slug-resistant than the drop-chute types.*

*The 1937 Wurlitzer catalogue stressed the special lighting effects 'inspired by the mighty Niagara' on the model 412.*

*Wurlitzer counter model 61 on its original base. (Courtesy John Ioneri/photo by Elliot Kaufmann)*

# CHAPTER 8

## Rock-Ola

*'The name was always Rockola. People would say Rocko, Rockla. But I would say, no, Rock<u>ola.</u> So I got to put a hyphen in it.'*

DAVID C. ROCKOLA was born in Verden, Manitoba, Canada. When he was fourteen, he left school and got a job. He found work in different places as a mechanic and wound up with a coin-machine company. He was interested in this business because he saw that a young man could start out on his own without too much money. When he was twenty-three, he crossed over into the United States and opened a small operating business with two partners. It grew until they had routes in Missouri and Illinois with five thousand weighing machines. He was responsible for supervising the maintenance; he understood the technical side of the business and was able to improve the equipment with simple modifications. He learnt about operating and that was a good education.

Rockola was a manufacturer by temperament and gravitated towards that side of the business. By 1926, he knew all there was to know about weighing machines, so he started the Rock-Ola Scale Company. His first machine was called the 'Low Boy'. It was well styled, simple and reliable and he had no trouble selling it. In 1930, some of his customers were getting in a new coin-operated table game called 'pinball'. It was spreading rapidly and Rockola decided to move into it in a big way. He retooled and came out with the 'Juggleball'. He had everything out on the line and it was a flop. He couldn't sell any. This was Rockola's first major setback in his business career. The economy of the country was in chaos

and his creditors called a meeting. When I interviewed him, he put it this way:

'They demanded their money back or I would be put in the hands of the receivers. I told them, ''Gentlemen, you can close me down and you'll get back five cents in the dollar. But if you let me stay in business, you'll get back every cent I owe you''.'

He was given time, so he pushed ahead. He was now geared up for pinball, and everybody wanted pinball. He knew where he had gone wrong with the 'Juggleball' and wouldn't make the same mistake again.

During the next three years, he made sixty different games, including 'Lucky Strike', 'Jigsaw', and 'World Series'. He paid off his creditors and was now a major factor in the coin-machine industry. In 1934, he purchased a large factory complex in Chicago where, initially, he used the space to make furniture. But Rockola was looking ahead. Pingames were under attack and were being banned in some parts of the country. Certain manufacturers were making horizontal slot machines and calling them 'pinball'. There was a wave of righteous indignation over the machine that 'snatched pennies' from the poor and corrupted little children, and since the racketeers had been put out of work by repeal, they had moved into operating games. Considering all these things, Rockola may have decided that pinball was not a sound base for his growing empire.

'Prohibition had been repealed and bars were opening up all over. People needed cheap entertainment, and I got to thinking about music. At

David C. Rockola's first business premises.

The Smythe mechanism used in Rock-Ola equipment from 1935 to 1948.

Rock-Ola's 'Multi-selector' of 1935, with twelve sections.

The 'Rhythm King' of 1937.

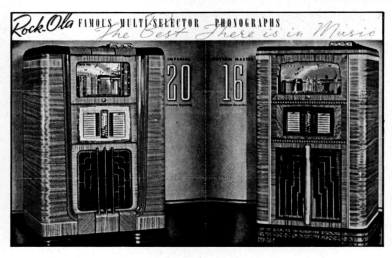

1936 'Regular' and 'Night Club' models.

Rock-Ola phonographs in walnut cabinets.

Production lines at the Rock-Ola plant in Chicago in the 1930s.

Rock-Ola publicity photograph for the 1940 counter model.

Publicity shot of the 'Multi-selector', 1935.

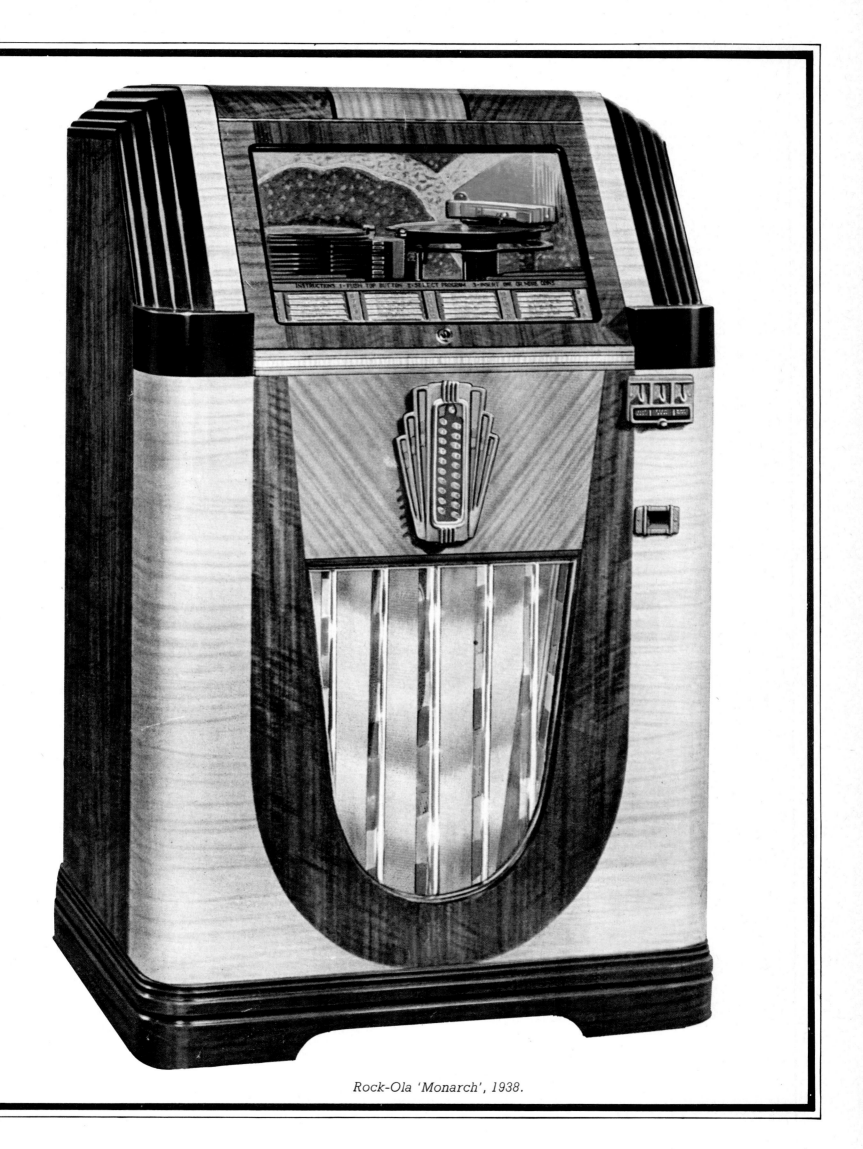

*Rock-Ola 'Monarch', 1938.*

about this time, a man called Smythe came to see me. He had been to Tonawanda, Jennings and Mills. He had a mechanism that could pick out a record from a stack, play it and replace it. They probably didn't want it because it needed a lot of work, but I could see that it was pretty sound, and anyway, I had been looking for one. So I went ahead and bought it. I had a good engineering team at the time. A man named Burnham, and . . . Swaggard. We worked on it for a long time and we got it right. I remember that Burnham was good. After he'd drunk a half of port, he could figure out ways to do anything.'

The rise of the young Rockola did not go unnoticed. He had already built up a reputation as one of the best engineers in the business. Now, he had moved into a three and a half block factory and was working on an advanced multi-selection record changer. It could mean only one thing.

In 1935, Wurlitzer had just got into its stride and was shipping 300 P12 phonographs a week. Seeburg was the only serious competitor and he was still a long way behind. Capehart knew that Wurlitzer had to stake its claim before the market stabilised, and he didn't want any newcomers rocking the boat. Especially Rockola, who was tough and looked as if he knew what he was doing.

Capehart called Rockola and suggested that they get together and talk things over. He agreed, and they fixed a day for Farny and Capehart to come over to Jackson Boulevard in Chicago.

Capehart did most of the talking. He explained to Rockola how things were in the juke box business: that it couldn't support more than one big manufacturer and anyway, the market was almost saturated.

.'They tried to sell me the idea of staying out of phonographs. They said they could make cabinets for my pinballs at the plant in Tonawanda. I listened for about one hour and finally I said, "Look, if you want, I can make cabinets for your phonographs in my new plant. As many as you want."

'The discussion got a little on the heavy side so I said, "Gentlemen, you asked for an interview with me. Now you are telling me how to run my business. We have nothing further to discuss." I opened the door and let them out.'

If Rockola had any doubts about moving into juke boxes, they were now dispelled. For Farny to come all this way just for a chat. it must be big.

Perhaps Capehart was figuring that Rockola could be browbeaten by the combination of his own threats and Farny's substance. But Rockola was as cool as ice, and now Capehart knew that he had to be stopped at all costs. Wurlitzer filed a suit against Rockola for $1,000,000 for infringement of a patent. Rockola counterclaimed for $2,000,000. The case dragged through the courts for several years and cost Rockola a half million dollars.

'The commissioner finally made his ruling during one of the conventions at the Sherman

*The coin mechanism is the kernel of the juke box, a two-inch square turnstile that harvests the millions of little coins that sustain an industry. They were being slugged to death until the 1930s and even then there was no real protection from J.D.s. The contemporary claim that this drop chute was 99 per cent slug proof was preposterous.*

**TONE QUALITY HOLDS BEST SPOTS**
Rock-Ola's superlative tone quality increases collections, draws crowds! Rich, clear, deep and powerful. Hear it for yourself! You'll say the tone is matchless.

**ROCK-OLA DELUXE AMPLIFIER**
Powerful! Simple! Only four tubes. Achieves richer and stronger tone without the distortion found in old style amplifiers using twice as many tubes.

**SCRATCHLESS REPRODUCTION**
Special unit in the Rock-Ola amplifier completely eliminates the disagreeable needle scratch of ordinary phonographs. Retains full range reproduction.

**DUAL MOTORS FOR EFFICIENCY**
Dual motors eliminate the need for clutches and other unnecessary parts. Control motor designed for changing of records only. Turntable motor also specially designed.

*More claims from Rock-Ola publicity.*

*Rock-Ola 'Luxury Light-up Super', 1939.*

The 1941 'Spectravox' could stand in the centre of the room, light and sound being emitted from the bowl on top. The tallest juke box ever built, very few were made and models are extremely rare today.

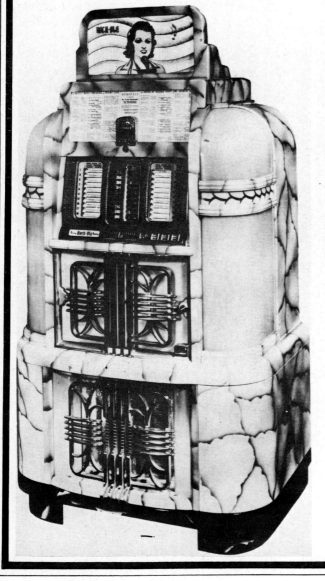

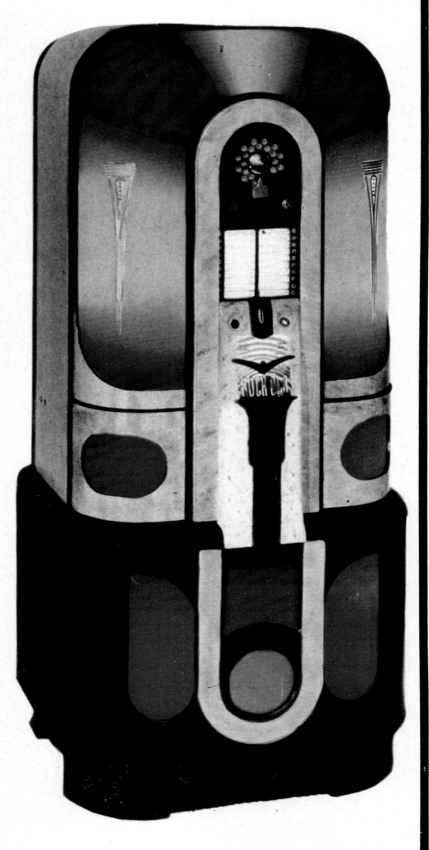

Above: The 'Premier' model had a short production run because of the war. This is also very rare today

Left: 'Dedicate a song to your friends' – Rock-Ola's version of the 'Mystic Music' telephone system, 1940.

*Rock-Ola 'Luxury Light-up'. (Acme Attractions)*

Hotel. We were all there. I got the result ahead of time and knew that we had won. Capehart came up to me and said, "Why don't you go over to Farny and work out a deal to pay him a royalty and take out a licence."

'We were walking down the hall, I said, "Capehart, that's not a bad idea."

'He didn't know that I had in my pocket notification that the commissioner had ruled in favour of Rock-Ola and that the twelve-play mechanism was the property of Smythe.'

Smythe in the meantime had sold the mechanism to Rock-Ola for a fixed sum payable over three years and was now out of a job. The Mills Novelty Company needed a new record changer and asked him to work for them; he designed the mechanism which was used in the 'Throne of Music' and the 'Empress'.

Rockola was not actually a threat to Wurlitzer's hegemony during the pre-war period, but he did account for more sales than any of the three manufacturers. Rockola claims that he designed all of his early juke boxes.

'I engaged different designers for the multi-selector, but they made the cabinets in such a way that they interfered with the mechanical side. So I went out to the market and found the nicest radio cabinet I could set my eyes on. I took it back to the shop and said, "Change this, change that. . ."'

David C. Rockola was a mogul in the real sense of the word. He ran his business singlehanded and his forceful personality is stamped on the products and the organisation of his company. In the industry, he was never considered a front runner, but he has proved to be the long-distance runner. When Seeburg and AMI sold out to large consortia, he retained control. When Mills and Wurlitzer found the going too rough and folded, he held on.

'We have had many propositions to sell stock. Sometimes six in a month. But I took an interest in what I was doing. I liked the fact that we controlled our own destiny. When we wanted to do something, we went ahead and did it. Our top people know that they have the freedom to use what ability they've got. A couple of years back [1973], things got very bad. We took drastic steps. We froze certain items and froze salaries. It put a lot more work on my shoulders. Nothing happened without my approval. Now my two sons are running the business. They've given me an office up here to keep me out of the way.'

Rockola was the last of the 'big five' to start manufacturing juke boxes. His timing was immaculate; he waited until the worst of the Depression had passed, but while there was still time to exploit the positive effects of repeal on the juke box market. If he had jumped in two or three years earlier, he would have found things a lot different, as Capehart, Seeburg, Mills and AMI had learned to their cost.

*Rock-Ola 'Dial-a-tune' wall box, 1941.*

*The same 'Luxury Light-up' as on the previous page, prior to restoration. (Burstein/Krivine)*

# CHAPTER 9

## Seeburg in the 1930s

DURING THE 1930s, Seeburg was a weak competitor. Rockola had entered the business eight years later than he, in 1935, and yet was shipping more phonographs in the period up to World War Two. From 1927 to 1934, Seeburg manufactured the 'Audiophone' series. These machines were very similar in operation to the Mills equipment. The ferris wheel mechanism required a lot of space and these early juke boxes were, of necessity, very broad. They were equipped with the latest electrical amplification and dynamic speakers and sold well during this period. By 1929, Seeburg felt that he had made the right decision in leaving pianos for phonographs.

In that year when the collapse came, the demand for automatic phonographs fell drastically and like AMI, Seeburg went into receivership and began looking about for new products to manufacture. During the next three years, he managed to keep one step ahead of his creditors by diversifying his interests. In the meantime, the company had been developing a new mechanism which was invented by a man called Wilcox. It was not unlike Capehart's 'Orchestrope', stacking ten records with a two-inch gap between each disc for the tone arm to slip in and play the record that had been selected. This phonograph was tall and slim, and the initial orders were good. But, ironically, a similar disaster overtook Seeburg as had befallen Capehart several years earlier. Operators started sending their equipment back to the factory because it was jamming up. The engineering department took the machines apart and discovered that the spindle on which the records were stacked had warped fractionally; the steel from which it was made had not been pre-stressed as a result of an error in the engineering department.

This is the juke box manufacturer's worst nightmare. Such an error would normally be fatal, but in 1934, the market was so strong that Seeburg

*Seeburg's 1934 model. The spindle warped – an expensive mistake.*
*(Courtesy K. Baxter)*

was able to regain his stride. They had a contingency in the Freborg mechanism which had been in the factory for several months undergoing development. This was incorporated into the Seeburg models for 1935 and the factory was back in full production.

J. P. Seeburg was now in his sixties and his son, Noel Marshall Seeburg, was beginning to take over the reins. Justus had been a highly successful manufacturer of player-pianos but had made the transition to phonographs with difficulty. Noel, however, was completely at home with the new electro-mechanical technologies and had inherited his father's drive and business ability; he soon began to make his presence felt in the organisation. He brought new talent into the company: M. W. Kenney, a bright young engineer, Nils Miller, an industrial designer and Henry Roberts, who became sales manager. Under his control, the company started to lay emphasis on two special areas: a much closer working relationship with the distributors and extensive research of the field in technology. He determined that these were the essential ingredients for a successful phonograph manufacturer and this was the way that Wurlitzer could be challenged.

Meyer Parkoff was a Wurlitzer distributor in New York in the mid-1930s who switched to Seeburg. According to Parkoff,

'Its [Seeburg's] mechanical performance was being approved by the operators. They all liked the way the machine was built. They had the "Gem", the "Crown", "Plaza", "Casino", "Regal", "Classic" and few other models I don't recall. I don't know what the reasons were that we went to Seeburg at that particular time – it's a little too far back for me to recall it. I think Seeburg had more flair for the commercial aspect of the juke box than Wurlitzer did at that time. They came out with interesting models. Very juke-boxy, if I may call it that, which means lots of lights, a lot of plastic. The design of the equip-

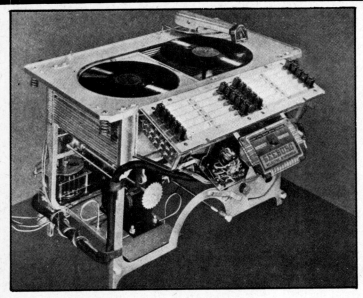

*The Freborg mechanism with sliding trays, used from 1936 to 1948. The number of selections was increased from ten to twenty. (Courtesy K. Baxter)*

*Carl Freborg, the mechanism's inventor.*

*Above and below: Two versions of the Seeburg's 'Symphonola', 1936.*

The 'Symphonola Classic' of 1938 was the first light-up juke box in the industry. (Burstein/Krivine)

ment was quite appealing to the public and to the location owner. And in addition, the equipment was engineered to a more scientific system than the Wurlitzer piece of equipment. They were certainly appealing to the operators that bought them. They were simple to repair and kept working much better.'

Seeburg, which had been expanding production along with the other manufacturers, scored a valuable point in 1938. Miller had been experimenting with phenolics and had produced a juke box with transluscent plastic panels behind which were fixed low wattage bulbs. The effect was to make the phonograph glow. Manufacturers had striven to give their equipment drawing power by using veneers, steps and angles on the wooden cabinets. But this was the age of electricity and the light-up juke box was a breakthrough. When the 'Symphonola' classic was unveiled at the 1938 Convention at the Sherman Hotel in Chicago, it stopped the show. Rockola, Wurlitzer and AMI went straight back to their factories and restyled their 1938 models. Tom Baxter, specifications engineer for Seeburg recalls that 'it was so popular that we went ahead and made universal cabinets for all the operators who wanted a light-up. Boy, we sold a lot of those cabinets.'

But Wurlitzer was soon producing models that far surpassed those of Seeburg in illumination and style. Seeburg was directing its main efforts to give the operators something that the other manufacturers didn't have. In 1939, they introduced the 'Wall-O-Matic'. It was a wall-box to be placed in booths, on walls and on counters, remote from the master phonograph. It offered the patrons a choice of twenty selections and operated through a multi-wire cable (one connection per selection) which Kenney called 'the wireless signalling system'. It transmitted the patron's choice from the wall-box to the phonograph by radio frequency signals conducted over power wiring. This permitted another novelty in the 'Play-Boy', a selection box on wheels that could be taken round a restaurant from table to table. In 1940, a concept similar to Rock-Ola's 'mystic music' was introduced. It was a system that resembled Pathe's Salon du Phonographie. About fifty phonographs in an area were connected by telephone wires to a central station. The station contained a record library, several turntables and one or more female 'jockeys'. The customer in any one of the taverns had a choice of 250 records in addition to the twenty selections offered by the master phonograph. By speaking into a mouth-piece, he could ask the young lady for any record on the supplementary list and once he had deposited his coin, the music would be piped through on to the juke box sound system. This was a novel innovation but it was still not successful. It would appear that in 1940, the public were satisfied with twenty selections.

Seeburg were trying hard to break out, but they were not hitting the target. They were, however, exhibiting a restless energy and a willingness to

The 'Universal' cabinet for operators who wanted the glow effect. (Courtesy K. Baxter)

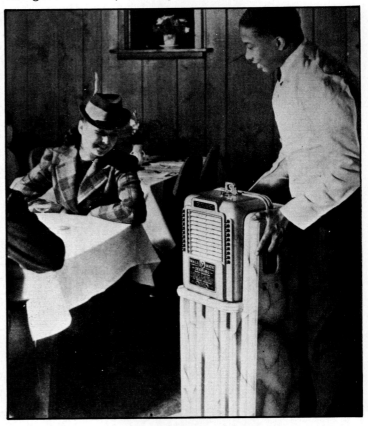

The 'Wall-o-matic' was wheeled from table to table so that patrons could make their selections without getting up. It was used in the better locations. (Courtesy K. Baxter)

try out new ideas which marked them out from their competitors, and which, within ten years, would project the company into the position of leadership in the juke box industry.

*Two studies of the Seeburg 'Symphonola Regal' of 1940. (Main picture Burstein/Krivine, inset courtesy Smithsonian Institution)*

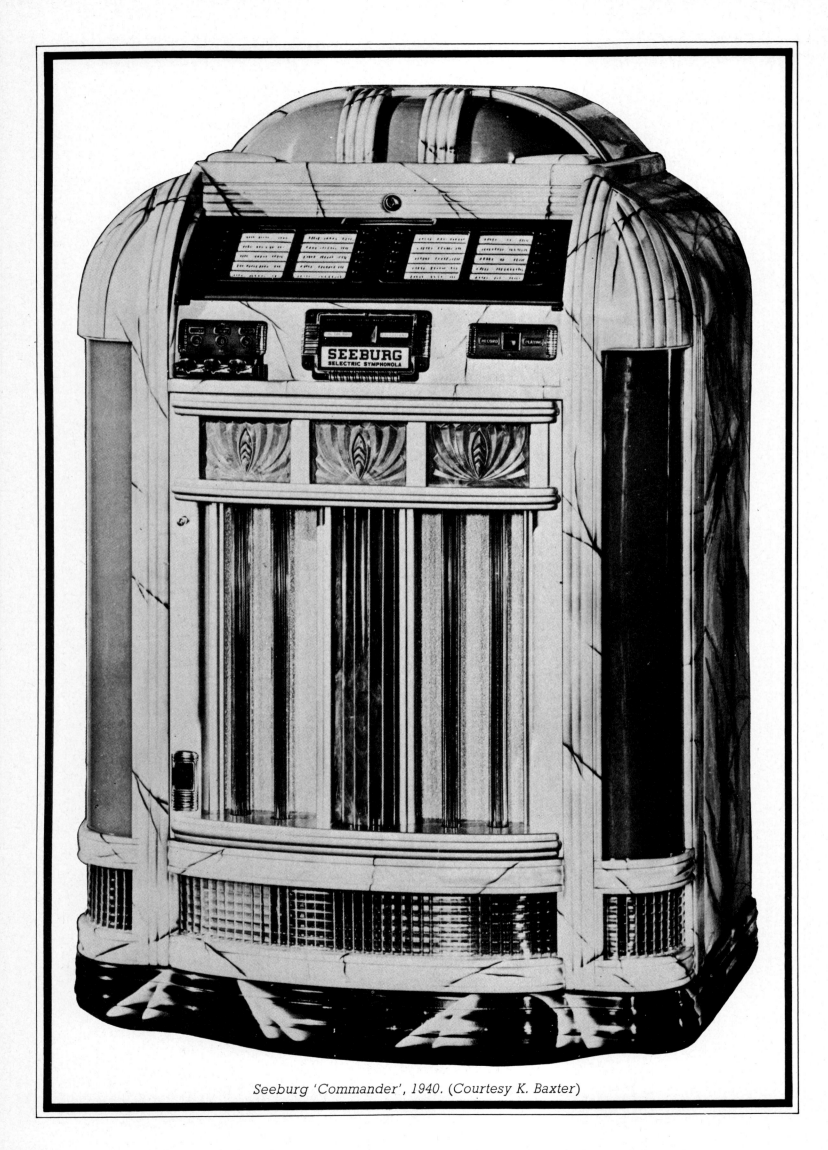

*Seeburg 'Commander', 1940. (Courtesy K. Baxter)*

*The Seeburg 'Playboy' of 1941 is very rare today. (Courtesy K. Baxter)*

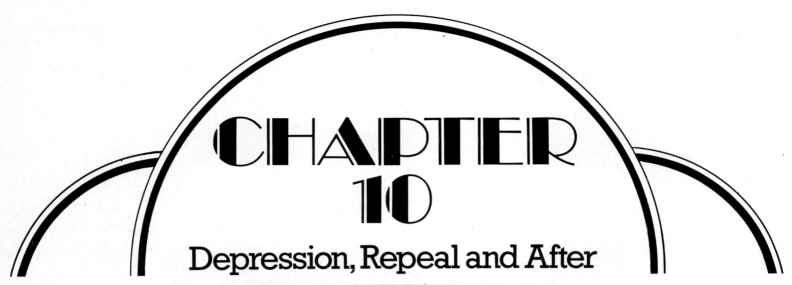

# CHAPTER 10

## Depression, Repeal and After

THE *New York Times* index of the 25 industrial stocks which early in 1924 had stood at 110, climbed by January 1929 to 338 and by September to 452. By mid-November, the index had fallen to 225. During the next four years, the Amercian economy was paralysed and one quarter of the civilian work force was unemployed.

That period is characterised by historians as one of universal frustration and despair; men standing in bread lines, sleeping in doorways, living in 'Hoovervilles', children hungry and shoeless, and farmers, having sold their homes, their lands and mortgaged their crops, still without enough money to live by. But this is by no means a complete picture. It has been known for a nation to be at war, its men being killed in their thousands,

*An AMI 'Streamliner' from the late 1930s. (Courtesy* Oui *magazine)*

yet for those living at a safe distance behind the front line, life continues almost as if nothing had changed. There were such paradoxes in the America of the 1930s, and nowhere were they more pronounced than in the field of entertainment.

Busby Berkely was a choreographer turned film director who worked in Hollywood at this time. He did not allow poverty and hopelessness to intrude into his work. In fact, he went to the other extreme, and filled his films with gaiety, wealth and splendour *ad absurdium*. The more frivolous it was, the bigger the box office; the public, at least those with the price of a theatre ticket,

wanted to have a good time.

Speakeasies were not adversely affected by the Depression. They provided booze and entertainment to the many Americans who wanted it. These were some of the earliest juke box locations. People didn't risk arrest and imprisonment to listen to Mozart or 'potted-palm' music on the radio, and a mechanical brass band was not quite in keeping with the surroundings. They wanted to hear jazz and country music, and if there wasn't a live band, they played the phonograph. The club owner liked juke boxes because they were relatively small and could be moved quickly if ever the need arose.

They were also good in candy stores, poolhalls, drug stores and restaurants. At a time when the disposable income of a large proportion of the population was measured in nickels and dimes, it helped to circulate what little there was. It was good for the location owner because it supplemented his income and the music attracted customers; you didn't hear too many phonographs in those days. The operators were able to get by, even when the takings were low, because the equipment was cheap (compared to a piano-player, for example).

Once Roosevelt had been voted to power, everyone knew that repeal of prohibition was just a matter of time. His 'happy days are here again' campaign and his broad infectious grin raised the spirits of America.

AMI's 'Singing Tower'. 'I bought a string of ''Singing
Towers'' before the war. Terrible machine, I couldn't get
them to work. The guy I sold them to made a fortune
with them,' says operator Dick Steinberg.
(Courtesy Oui magazine)

'I recall exactly the day prohibition ended. I went into a restaurant that started serving booze. It was such a strange feeling 'cause I started drinking in speaks. I didn't know about open drinking, to go off the street and order a drink without having an arm on your shoulder. I'd gotten used to the idea of being disreputable.'

(from Studs Terkel's *Hard Times*)

Taverns opened up on almost every street corner. For every speakeasy that disappeared, four or five bars opened, and overnight there were thousands of potential juke box locations. From an estimated 25,000 phonographs in 1933, by 1937 there were 225,000. This increase was three times the national average of 'durables', and is some indication of their enormous popularity.

The juke boxes were still playing jazz, but now in a much decaffeinated form, as recorded by such artists as Vincent Lopez, Paul Whiteman, the Dorsey Brothers and Benny Goodman, the 'King of Swing'.

'The Music Goes Round and Round' sold 100,000 copies in 1936 and that hadn't happened since the 1920s. Decca were putting their weight behind 'popular' music and had signed up several of Brunswick's 75c artists: Guy Lombardo, the Mills Brothers, Arthur Tracy, and the Rhythm Boys – one of whom was Bing Crosby. In fact Crosby was so unbelievably popular that many of the so-called record stations, those which depended almost entirely upon records for broadcasting, found it expedient to feature programmes of Crosby records twice a day and sometimes at an even higher frequency.

By 1939, juke boxes were consuming approximately 30 million records per year. Gelatt reckons that 'for record companies, the juke box served the double function of buyer and seller. Millions of records were purchased because they had been heard the night before on a juke box.'

In the same year, 'Beer-barrel Polka', which was played on every juke box in America, sold 300,000 copies. The retail price of a Decca record was 35c. The operators were able to obtain these records direct from the wholesalers. They could use the same record on several of their machines before it was finally scrapped; thus the earning power of a single hit that cost them 19c or less could be as much as $10.

Like the music, the public had changed too. Most of the nickels were now being dropped by white teenagers and in many instances the juke box was considered suitable for family entertainment. The operators encouraged this tendency; not only was it good for business, but it gave them respectability. Ever since the racketeers had moved into the 'slots' (one-armed-bandits), the coin industry had had a monkey on its back. It was said that when repeal came, the hoods began operating the amusement equipment, such as pinball and phonographs. Whether or not this was true, it was a tough business to be in. The word 'juke box' itself was still bad, though. It was like Hooverville and speakeasy all rolled into one

*Bing Crosby, 'King of the Juke Boxes'.*

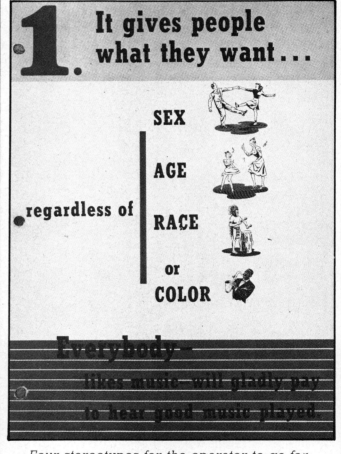

*Four stereotypes for the operator to go for.*

and what was even worse, it sounded black. The industry began to take a look at its image. During one of his harangues to the distributors, Capehart urged them to 'raise their status from mere coin-operators to that of "music merchants"'. Capehart always referred to his equipment as the 'phonograph'. During the 1950s, Seeburg tried to educate their public to call the equipment a 'music system'. To the distributors, they were always 'pieces of equipment' and in the South, operators called them 'piccolos' or 'wurtelisers'. But the public liked juke box and it stuck. It is ironic to note that in 1973 the Wurlitzer Company, in a final effort to revive their phonograph division, attempted to recapture the magic of the 1940s with a 'nostalgia' model; written on the front glass was 'juke box'. But it was too late.

*Gabel product circa 1936. (Courtesy John Ioneri/photo by Elliot Kaufmann)*

# CHAPTER 11
## The War Years

WHEN WAR in the Pacific became inevitable, there were public figures in Japan and elsewhere who believed that America had grown soft in its occidental luxury, and lacked the will to fight. Their sad miscalculation is now a matter of history; not only did the American people rise to the occasion, but as a result of the war, achieved feats of industrial production that had never been dreamed possible. Unemployment effectively disappeared as all available resources, human and non-human, were sucked into the war machine. In 1943, the American economy was running at maximum capacity. By 1945, the world was at its feet.

*Seeburg's 'Hi Tone'. 'This machine was way ahead of its time because the speakers were at the top. But it was a difficult piece of equipment from the operators' point of view because they had to get down on their knees to repair the mechanism.' – Meyer Parkoff, Seeburg distributor.*

As far as the automatic phonograph was concerned, the first shot was fired by Donald M. Nelson, priorities director of the Office of Production Management.

'The government prohibited today the production of coin-operated gambling machines after 1 February, and simultaneously told manufacturers of juke boxes and some other coin-operated devices to curtail their output by 75 % by the same date. The order . . . was the most drastic limitation yet placed on civilian industry because of shortage of materials needed in defense production.' (*New York Times*, 11 December 1941)

Juke boxes were high on the list of the nation's least essential products. By the spring of 1942, no more phonographs were being made. The great factories of Chicago, North Tonawanda and Grand Rapids were in the process of retooling for the manufacture of equipment that would be entertaining no one. War fever was everywhere and people were glad of an opportunity to pitch in, especially if it didn't involve getting killed. The manufacturers now went looking for Government contracts for the production of munitions.

Rock-Ola made rifles and ammunition boxes. At the peak of production, they were turning out 2500 M30s and 1000 ammunition boxes per day; the factory was now on three eight-hour shifts. Wurlitzer made components for aircraft, de-icing equipment, range finders, proximity fuses and electronic devices for tanks and the signal corps. After hostilities ceased, the company continued producing for the Pentagon and was very active in this area during the Korean War. In the 1960s, Wurlitzer developed a thermal battery that was used in the Minute Man project and also in a Bendix communications system that is, at the time of writing, sitting on the moon. Nicholas of Schilback had come a long way.

Homer E. Capehart, recently elected to the Senate as Republican representative for Indiana, returned to Fort Wayne to organise the Packard Corporation for war work. By 1943, the factory was employing two thousand men and women and at the end of the war, Packard was awarded no less that five Army and Navy 'E' (excellence) awards for its contribution to the war effort.

N. Marshal Seeburg describes how his father responded to the new circumstances.

This 1942 Farm Security Administration photo by
John Collin shows teenagers in Richwood, West
Virginia, listening to music from a Wurlitzer 850.
(Courtesy Library of Congress)

In the mood. (Time-Life Picture Agency)

Rock-Ola reminds the operators that it is still around; after it has helped beat the Japs, it will be back in
production with juke boxes.

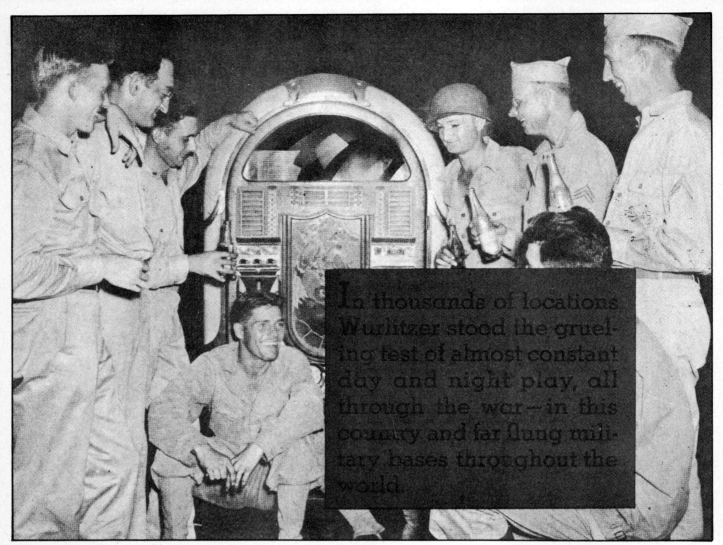

Wurlitzer publicity, 1946.

*Everybody's happy. (Courtesy M. Trussell)*

*Wurlitzer publicity, 1943. (Courtesy M. Trussell)*

'When the war came along, most of our competitors took whatever they could find. We were a little more selective; we stayed in the field of electro-mechanics. We made the "Intervalometer" – timed release of bombs – and we had a large research department. When the war was over, we were ahead in electro-mechanical technologies and were working to much higher tolerances.'

The engineering department had grown from seventy to one hundred and thirty technicians, some of whom were top university graduates. Seeburg also continued with defence work after the war and although this was not particularly profitable, it enabled Seeburg to make experiments that would not otherwise have been possible.

There were many changes inside the factories that were directly the result of the new circumstances. The old work force had been broken up when the young men were drafted into the services; their places were filled by whoever was available, and soon there were a lot of new faces on the shop floor. The relaxed, secure atmosphere of pre-war days had been replaced by frantic production deadlines as the factory worked round the clock. There were no more coach outings and social clubs for the employees and the work became dehumanised. The close links that had existed between management and labour were broken and the trade unions, for the first time, gained a foothold in these companies. By the end of the war, the Electrical Workers' Union had a presence throughout the manufacturing industry, and the process was an irreversible one.

The war had turned the country's social life upside down. It created an atmosphere of uncertainty; the young men were overseas, some of them never to return. Those who stayed home worked long unsocial hours in the armaments factories alongside 'Rosie the Rivetter'. Many of the young women had enlisted and had accepted postings wherever they were needed. There was very little home life at this time; people wanted to escape from their anxieties as they had done during the Depression, but now they had money to spend. They could afford to eat out in restaurants and the taverns were always full. Their numbers were augmented by servicemen on home leave, itinerant workers and soldiers from the local bases. There was a spirit that drew people together and one felt less inhibited about dancing with a stranger or having a few extra beers. It was for many a carefree and romantic period and the desire for music was self-evident. In these circumstances, the juke box was a focal point in lives of both civilians and conscripts, and many machines had been shipped overseas by the military to boost the morale of the soldiers in their encampments in Europe and the Far East. The tall stack of records with gentle melodies and sentimental refrains, encased in the warm, glowing wooden cabinets with their solid American names were reassuring and omnipresent.

For the operators, it was a bonanza. Those were the best years in the history of the industry

D. Steinberg, an operator in the 1930s, comments:

'When the war came, I enlisted. I was thirty-five years old but that didn't matter because I knew that I had to go. In a way it was a pity. If I was operating in World War Two, I'd have to be a dope not to make a million dollars. They were selling 750Es for over $900 apiece. You couldn't get hold of equipment.'

Meyer Parkoff explains that

'It was very difficult for the distributor in those particular days because there was no new equipment to sell. We would buy up a route, say, over in Pennsylvania. We would rip off all the locations that didn't pay, that were very poor stops, and bring the equipment into the State [New York] and get a new price for it in the City. The balance we would sell to another operator. We sold parts, serviced and refurbished machines . . . we had to stay in business. In my experience, we bought out routes from men who needed to sell and we gave them a good price. I really can't remember what routes went for in those days but I think, if I recall correctly, that it was twenty times the weekly income plus the cost of the equipment. Some of them made special cabinets at that time, but we thought it was not a practical idea – it was too costly.'

There were not enough machines to go round. Operators pulled old P10s and 'multi-selectors' out of their cellars and put them out to work. Thousands of 'universal' cabinets were sold and Wurlitzer's 'Victory' was used in the best locations throughout America. Some operators employed the 'Mystic Music' system of one juke box as a central source of music, piped into the other locations over telephone lines. In 1945, Wurlitzer was planning a campaign to launch a ten cent and three-for-a-quarter play pricing although Seeburg was opposed to this idea. The 400,000 juke boxes were insufficient to meet demand and some observers were prompted to remark that by the end of the war, there would be a need for 800,000 in the US alone.

Those operators who had the equipment could write their own contracts. They were able to ask for a larger percentage of the increased takings, and new locations were opening up every month. In 1941, the record makers were enjoying a boom period with 127,000,000 sales in the twelve months before the outbreak of war. According to Billboard's Harold Humphrey, over half were sold to juke box operators. 'Many top-name band leaders went on record as preferring a hit recording to all the air-time they could get.'

However, at the beginning of 1942, the Government prohibited the use of shellac in records. Burma, which was the source of the compound, had been cut off by the Japanese and all existing stocks were requisitioned by the military for their own requirements. The record companies immediately announced that they would pay for any old records – even if they were chipped – in order to recycle the shellac. In August 1942, they had an even more serious problem on their hands.

James Caesar Petrillo, President of the American Federation of Musicians, claimed that the juke box was partly responsible for 60% of its 138,000 members being out of work. He called it affectionately 'Scab Number One'.

Petrillo could remember the days when thousands of restaurants and dance halls had employed their own ensembles and was determined that, even if he couldn't turn the clock back, he would at least force the record companies to share some of their profits with the musicians. He had been working for a royalty agreement with the recording companies for many years but without success. Now, at the end of his tether, he called a national strike that went into effect on 1 August. Roland Gelatt explains:

'An order went out to every local in the country instructing union members to refuse all recording engagements after 31 July. The edict, which applied equally to Leopold Stokowski and Benny Goodman, was meticulously obeyed by a well disciplined and all-powerful union.'

For two years Columbia and RCA Victor held out and during that period there were no new recordings for the juke boxes to play. The public had to be satisfied with whatever the record companies could dig out of their archives. When they eventually capitulated, so eager was the public for something new, that the first recordings, an album of songs from *Oklahoma* (admittedly a good musical) sold 1,300,000 copies and was to be heard on every juke box.

When the war ended, the juke box industry had cause for great optimism. Their product was more popular than ever, the demand was still increasing, and soon, exciting new models would be coming on to the market. They could barely wait.

*Publicity for the new 1943 Wurlitzers.* (*Courtesy M. Trussell*)

# CHAPTER 12

## Wurlitzer Succumbs to Seeburg's Secret Weapon

WHEN THE manufacturing restrictions were lifted at the end of the war, it was a race to bring new equipment on to the market. Fred Osborne of Wurlitzer says that 'all the operators had five-year-old phonos and were hungry for new ones. It was a standing joke in the industry that you could sell a packing case if it had a coin slot in it.'

*The turning point – the Seeburg M100A.*

Seeburg were first in with their model P146. In this series (146/7/8, the last numerals denoting the years) Seeburg had a low-cost, reliable and unusual-looking phonograph. It had the faithful Freborg twenty-selection mechanism and the title strips (the small cards indicating the songs and artists available) were positioned inside the selector buttons.

Parkoff said,

'We used to call it the "ash can" because it had a red lid that opened up. You never heard it before? It may have been a good working model, but it wasn't an attractive machine; the ops didn't like it at all.'

Steinberg commented,

'I went into the "turret" thing which I shouldn't have, but they were the only phonographs available at the time. They had put aside a lot of money and parts and when the war ended, they went straight into production. It wasn't a successful machine, but they sold a lot. There was nothing else to buy.'

This model had one major drawback in that the record changer could not be viewed, because the Freborg mechanism was itself encased in a steel frame. The visibility of the moving parts was a strong selling point for the public, and Wurlitzer, Rock-Ola and AMI had capitalised on this feature. The general antipathy towards the P146 brought home to Seeburg the need to change the Freborg for an 'open-type' mechanism.

AMI, who during the immediate pre-war years had produced a series of elegant and stylish phonographs culminating in the 'Singing Tower', had received word that the fashion was for bright juke boxes. The model 'A', as well as being the best seller to date, was the most garish juke box ever designed. Six feet high, it was a mass of amorphous moulded translucent plastic with a tasteless cluster of outsize 'jewels' at the base, and one is forced to conclude that the designer was much addicted to ice-cream. In the AMI 'B' that followed in 1947, the only concession that the designer was willing to make to the sensibilities of the more conservative elements of the American public was in scaling the machine down to life size and removing the jewellery.

Paul Fuller had, in 1940, emerged as the design leader of the industry and Wurlitzer had come to regard him as one of their principal assets. Fred Osborne recalls that, 'During the war, the company had not spent a cent on tools, so Paul was allowed to shoot the works. The box was full of die castings, formed plastics and other things.' Wurlitzer expected him to produce a beautiful phonograph and they were not disappointed. The model 1015 is the best-known and best-loved juke box. The front of the machine was one unbroken arc of moving light. Bubbles rose from four invisible sources at the base and converged at the top of the full arch, while two multi-coloured fluorescent tubes revolved slowly within the two columns bathing the juke box and its immediate surroundings in a soft warm glow, red, now blue, now green.

When Mike Hammergren unveiled this creation to the delighted group of distributors, he proceeded to announce that a very special campaign had been prepared, a promotion more ambitious than anything that had ever been attempted. 'At

*A Seeburg P147 'washing machine' awaiting restoration. (Acme Attractions)*

*AMI Model 'A' of 1946-8, known affectionately as the 'mother of plastic'. (Acme Attractions)*

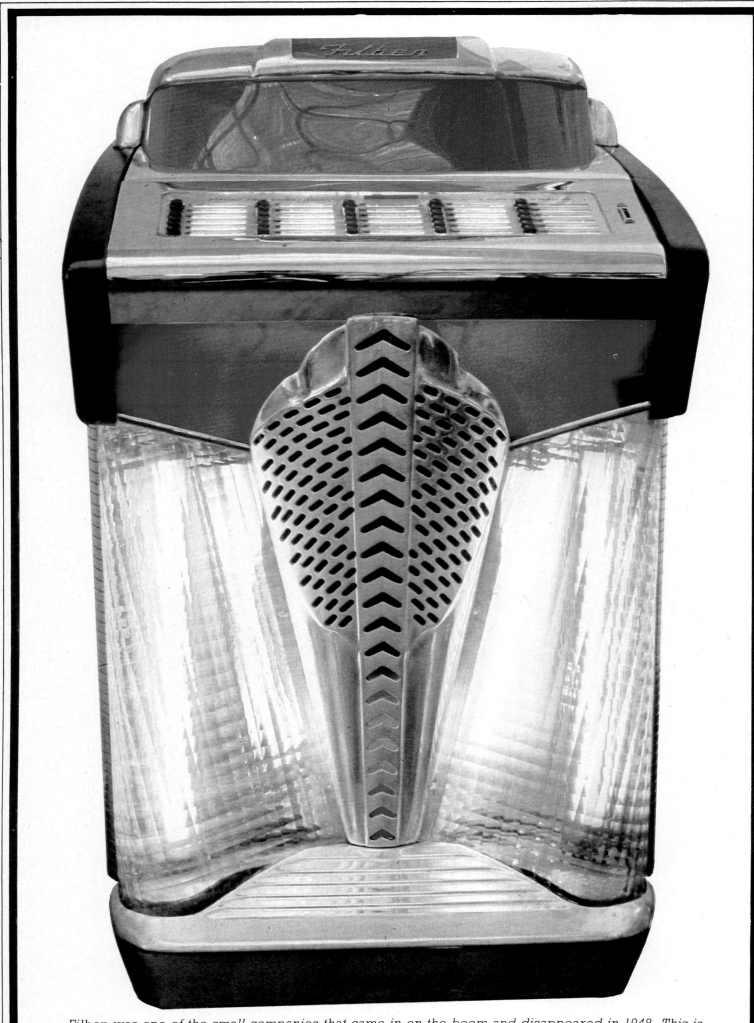

Filben was one of the small companies that came in on the boom and disappeared in 1948. This is the 'Maestro', built like a locomotive. (Acme Attractions)

that time, they came out with an advertising campaign that was unbelievable. Every conceivable item from napkins, table tops, cocktail sticks, mats, decals, signs . . . unbelievable!' remarked Dick Steinberg.

Illuminated signs with the new Wurlitzer 'Johnny One-note' logo were to be placed outside locations to beckon the public to Wurlitzer music. They went in bars, diners, hotels and pool halls – into every place that Americans went for their recreation and entertainment. It was intended to equate location music with the name Wurlitzer and the image of the 1015 was the central theme of the campaign.

Rockwellian illustrations of the 1015, surrounded by an adulatory group of contented Americans appeared in full-page colour advertisements in the best national magazines. Large billboards on highways throughout the country proclaimed the message 'Wurlitzer is juke box'. It was mounted on the same scale and in the same idiom as one of Coca-Cola's periodic assaults on the public's consciousness. In addition to the fact that the 1946 model was quite superb, there was still, in the summer of that year, a strong demand for new equipment in a market that had expanded considerably over the past five years; success, therefore, was assured. 56,000 1015s were shipped from North Tonawanda in 18 months, the biggest juke box of all time.

In taking its case directly to the public, Wurlitzer had made a radical departure from normal juke box practice. Promotional activity had always been directed at the operator and location owner through the medium of the specialist journals like *Billboard*, *Cashbox* and *Automatic Age*. Yet however successful this campaign might have been, the public were not able to express their preference for Wurlitzer in the normal way. They could not go out and buy the product as if it were an automobile, a soft drink or chewing gum. Nor could they be expected to go out looking for Wurlitzers (as opposed to Seeburgs, or Filbens) in the same way they might go to see a particular movie. Nevertheless, so great was America's awareness of juke boxes at this time, that the decision of where to eat, drink and dance could actually be influenced by the type of juke box that the location offered. Therefore, 1946 could be taken as the year in which the juke box had the greatest influence on American society. In any event, Wurlitzer was widely diversified in the field of musical instruments, and all of its divisions stood to benefit from this campaign.

Fuller followed in 1947 with the model 1100. It was conceived as 'ultra modern'. The brochure reads,

'The 1100 Is More Fun To Watch!
Because its great plastic panoramic *sky-top turret window* will draw people like a magnet. Your customers will watch the mechanism work. Now, as never before, this wide open bomber-nose window gives them an unobstructed view. It puts them right where you want them – next to the coin slide.'

The juke box was streamlined to a subtle point at the top of the arch, the light was harder and the selector buttons were redesigned to give the customer the sensation that he was even more in control. It was part spaceship.

The model 1080 of 1946 had been designed with more conservative locations in mind, though. Wurlitzer suggested that

'Location owners, who feel that a period design best lends itself to their decorative scheme, will prefer the Wurlitzer Colonial Model 1080A . . . The graceful colonial-style cabinet . . . is a period masterpiece, rich in old world charm. Its illuminated mirror plastics have the glow and sparkle of fine cut glass. An early American lyre inspired the styling of its colourful grill. And its visible record-changer background reproduces a famous 18th century painting.'

Almost 80,000 phonographs were shipped in the 18 months ending December 1947, over 70% of total output by the industry, and Wurlitzer was riding on the crest of a wave. But this was to be short-lived.

The economy passed through a mild recession as the nation reverted back from guns to butter. The return of the soldiers to civilian life swelled the ranks of the unemployed. The atmosphere was one of anti-climax. America had enjoyed her moments of victory and now there was nothing to follow. People had slowly to pick up the pieces and return to the old routines. Young couples began raising families and home life came back into

*Homer E. Capehart, Senator for Indiana, couldn't get juke boxes out of his blood. At the end of the war, he was back in production with 5000 Packard 'Pla-mors'.*

*The classic juke box – Wurlitzer's 1015, of which some 56,000 were made. (Burstein/Krivine)*

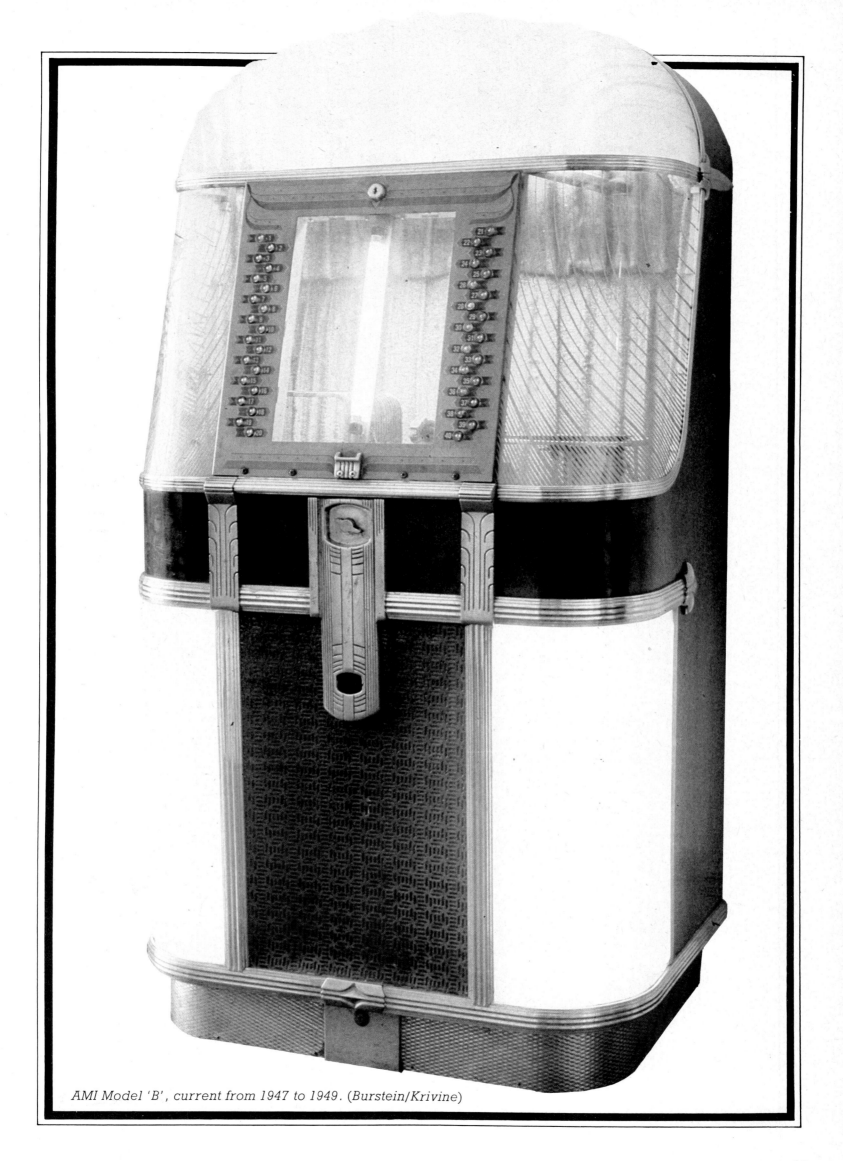

*AMI Model 'B', current from 1947 to 1949. (Burstein/Krivine)*

fashion as the processes of normalisation began. There was also the beginnings of a conservatism in American life that was vaguely hostile to nights out at the tavern. Under these circumstances, *Billboard's* estimate of 800,000 juke boxes was hopelessly awry.

Wurlitzer had also overestimated, expecting sales of the 1100 to equal that of its predecessor. Once the surplus had been made manifest, production was cut back drastically and the company announced a new credit deal for the operators to encourage them to buy the 1100 and 1080. Rock-Ola and Seeburg found themselves in similar straits, and they, too, were offering easy terms to the operators in order to clear stocks.

In 1946, several new companies had entered the field in the hope of making a killing; Filben produced the 'Maestro', Pantages had the 'Hollywood', and Keeny and H. C. Evans manufactured their own equipment.

Homer E. Capehart made a dramatic comeback with his Packard 'Pla-mor' and the 'Manhattan' counter model. He was faced with the intriguing problem of how to break into a market that he himself had sewn up for the big manufacturers. He had established the principle of distributorships, but in 1946 he had no such organisation himself. With some skill and great cunning, he announced to the industry that distributors were no longer necessary and that he, for one, would be selling equipment direct to the operators. But the ploy failed. In a recent interview, he estimated that about 5000 'Pla-mors' were shipped and added that he didn't think he'd made a profit.

The move by Packard climaxed a year of upheaval among the distributors as franchises were switched, territories were enlarged or split and changes among distributors averaged five per month. By 1948, operators were returning their 1100s to Hammergren with a perfunctory 'no thanks'. Filben and Pantages disappeared as suddenly as they had arrived and Mills, as we shall see in the next chapter, was gone. There was a glut of phonographs and the market had dried up.

The Scott Fellows Bill was going through Congress in 1948; it sought to end the exemption from copyright payments enjoyed by operators since 1909. Petrillo's powerful union was pressing for a share in some of the profits the juke box was earning from their music, and the operators were genuinely concerned about the future. If the principle of royalty payments was finally accepted, this would surely be the thin end of the wedge for them.

It was at this time that dire things were happening at Chateau Wurlitzer.

Capehart had been succeeded in 1938 by M. G. Hammergren. He had remained with the company for several months in order to show the new general sales manager the ropes and during the two remaining years of peace, Hammergren was carried along by the momentum of the superb organisation that Capehart had created during his five-year tenure. After the war, although Hammergren's advertising campaign had raised a few eyebrows, he was generally given credit for the tremendous success which Wurlitzer had enjoyed with the model 1015. However, when overproduction combined with the minor recession of 1947-8 to produce a glut of unwanted equipment, Hammergren was faced with his first major crisis.

The general sales manager is the kingpin of the industry. He must know what is happening in the field before it happens, and pass the information on to the designers and engineers. He has to decide when to increase output, when to cut back, when to introduce a new model, and what sort of equipment the operators will be looking for. During the 1930s, Capehart orchestrated the production and distribution of Wurlitzer's models and gave leadership to the entire industry. In 1937 he had anticipated an overproduction phase and skilfully avoided it. He always ensured that Wurlitzer was not left with unsold stock.

Hammergren, however, was not strictly speaking a juke box man. Before coming to North Tonawanda, he had been in the company's retailing division and had been given the job on the strength of his excellent record for selling pianos to the public. But phonographs were a different proposition. When the bottom fell out of the market in 1948 he was caught off balance. With 4000 1015s already in storage, hundreds of model 1100s were coming off the production line each week with no place to go. R. C. Rolfing called a halt to production and instigated an all-out effort to sell existing stock. At that time, all the manufacturers were experiencing difficulties, but none on the scale of Wurlitzer. From average sales of 35,000 units (taking an average from 1936 to 1947), only 7000 phonographs were shipped from North Tonawanda in 1948. Ultimately, the responsibility for this failure rests with the people who had selected Hammergren and to whom he was responsible. It is difficult to imagine N. Marshal Seeburg or David C. Rockola allowing such a thing to happen in their organisations, and it does raise serious doubts about the quality of the leadership at Wurlitzer in this period. Farny Wurlitzer cannot, however, be blamed for the

*Capehart receives a pat on the back from Uncle Sam for his part in the war effort. This did his new career no harm.*

*Rock-Ola 1426, 1947. (Acme Attractions)*

fact that the man whom he had hired didn't act according to his (Farny's) own high business principles.

Hammergren was fired in 1948; after his departure, he was the subject of an investigation by the Internal Revenue and it emerged that he had defrauded the Wurlitzer company out of $300,000 and the Federal Government out of $1 million. A $4000 cabin cruiser that he had received as a 'gift' from the Landsheft advertising company was sold in settlement of the debt (A. D. Palmer, who took over as general sales manager in 1949, recalls that when he arrived, his first job was to incinerate hundreds of thousands of dollars worth of advertising material that had been ordered but never distributed). As if the scandal and the financial crisis was not bad enough, there was yet another development that threatened the wounded manufacturer: In 1948, Seeburg unveiling a new juke box which was at least three years ahead of anything that was being produced in the industry. It was called the M100A.

The story of this development began in 1941 when an inventor called Ed Andrews came to see Mr Kenney at Seeburg. He had a record changer that stacked and played the records vertically. According to N. Marshall Seeburg, he was a difficult man to deal with and had been unable to sell his invention to the other people for this reason. But his father was keen on the mechanism and came to terms with the irascible inventor. Kenney remembers a different side to Andrews, and says 'he was a hard worker and a professional.' Kenney detailed a group of engineers to

*Illustration from a Wurlitzer advertisement which appeared in* Collier's, Look, Liberty *and the* Saturday Evening Post *in July 1946.*

*Wurlitzer's November and December 1946 ad for the glossies.*

*Rock-Ola distributor's ad in* Cashbox, *1947. Rock-Ola, like many manufacturers, supplied blocks for the logo and graphic designs themselves.*

*This ad appeared in February and March in several of the biggest magazines, including* True Confessions. *Note the girl in the centre – she appears in later Wurlitzer publicity.*

*It's what America's all about.*

*Ad illustration in* Life, Look, Red Book *and the* Saturday Evening Post, *January and February 1947.*

*Overleaf left: Wurlitzer pitch their advertising at the family.*

*Overleaf right: This ad hit the national magazines in the spring of 1946.*

# *After the Easter Parade...*

ALBERT DORNE

## *Musical Fun for Everyone*

Bright Easter finery. A smart Easter hat. Gay Easter flowers. It's every woman's right to glow with pride in the Easter parade. And, it's no woman's wish to go home and spend the rest of the day in the kitchen.

There's a hint for husbands here. Take the family out for dinner—where they have Wurlitzer Music. Your friends will be there with their families. All of you, young and old, will have fun talking, laughing and listening to tunes as stimulating as your first fresh breath of spring. The Rudolph Wurlitzer Company, North Tonawanda, New York. ★ ★ ★ See Phonograph Section of Classified Telephone Directory for names of Wurlitzer Dealers.

The *Sign of the Musical Note* identifies places where you can have fun playing a Wurlitzer.
➡

# "Oh Boy, they have WURLITZER MUSIC!"

## America's favorite nickel's worth of fun

All over America today, people in search of good entertainment at a reasonable price are learning to look for the Wurlitzer *Sign of the Musical Note.*

There you find Wurlitzer Music . . . 24 of the latest tunes played by the greatest bands in the land . . . for only a nickel a number. Pick your favorites from a musical menu of sweet numbers, jazz classics, hill billy hits, waltzes, fox trots, polkas.

You'll go home humming their haunting melodies, higher in spirit, happier at heart for having spent a pleasant musical interlude by spending only a few small coins. That's why Wurlitzer Music is nationally known as *America's Favorite Nickel's Worth of Fun.* The Rudolph Wurlitzer Company, North Tonawanda, New York.

The *Sign of the Musical Note* identifies places where you can have fun playing a Wurlitzer.

### THE NAME THAT MEANS *Music* TO MILLIONS

The music of Wurlitzer pianos, accordions, electronic organs, and juke boxes is heard " 'round the world." Wurlitzer is America's largest manufacturer of pianos all produced under one name . . . also America's largest, best known, manufacturer of juke boxes and accordions.

WURLITZER PHONOGRAPH MUSIC

commence development on the Andrews mechanism but their work was interrupted by the War.

As we have already seen, Seeburg had acquired a team of highly qualified young engineers for work on the military equipment and by the end of the War, when work was resumed on the Andrews mechanism, Kenney's department was working on ideas far ahead of the competition.

Carl T. McKelvy had joined the Seeburg team in 1943 as general sales manager. As a juke box salesman, he was second only to Capehart and was especially enthusiastic about the Andrews mechanism because he knew that the public was ready for a new kind of juke box. During the 1930s, Capehart had confidently asserted that 24 selections was as many as people would ever need. But in 1948, America was a different country. It had emerged from the War proud and prosperous and people were becoming size- and quantity-orientated. Cars, TVs, cities, incomes, everything was bigger and better than in the previous year; it had become a national compulsion. McKelvy was a very able salesman and understood the public's mood. He put his full weight behind the 100-selection mechanism where others might have wavered. He promoted the new juke box as the biggest, most sophisticated and therefore most desirable music system of the age. In reality, it still only played one record at a time and it sounded no different, but that was beside the point.

Nils Miller had been briefed to produce a cabinet that would reflect the revolutionary changes within. He therefore made a break with the curves and arches, the mellow lighted plastics and crafted wooden cabinets. It was now a square shape with sharp corners and tapering edges,

chromium trimmings and hard fluorescent light. It was not as strong a statement as its immediate successors, but the M100A was still a radically different juke box to anything that was being made at that time. In purely design terms, it was several years ahead of Detroit. It was a calculated risk that required a great deal of courage.

N. Marshall Seeburg recalls that

'They didn't bring out a new model every year; it was very expensive to tool up – eight to nine hundred thousand dollars . . . Given the capital structure of these companies, with the possible exception of Wurlitzer, it was not possible to do this on an annual basis. You gather all your strength together, bring out the new model and hope that it will last forever. Every time a new model was ready, we would hire a hotel and put on a four-day blast. Meanwhile the senior service executives were receiving instruction on the new features. Finally, the last thing was the price. The whole event was designed to soften the blow.'

When the M100A was unveiled to the distributors, it caused a sensation. Just to show the potential of the new system Kenney had built a 500-selection mechanism mounted on a frame. Such a juke box would have been as wide as a piano and hopelessly impractical but the distributors took the point.

This machine made all the others look like antiques. Many operators who had been faithful to Wurlitzer or Rock-Ola for several years now wanted the 'Selectomatic' for their best locations. As far as the public was concerned, in 1948 there was only one juke box; once they had played from a choice of 100, they would never settle for anything less. For the other manufacturers, already suffering as a result of over-production, this was all very depressing.

*The post-war 'Johnny-one-note' logo.*

*These pin-ups were used in Wurlitzer juke box locations.*

*Billboard advertising in 1946 (also overleaf).*

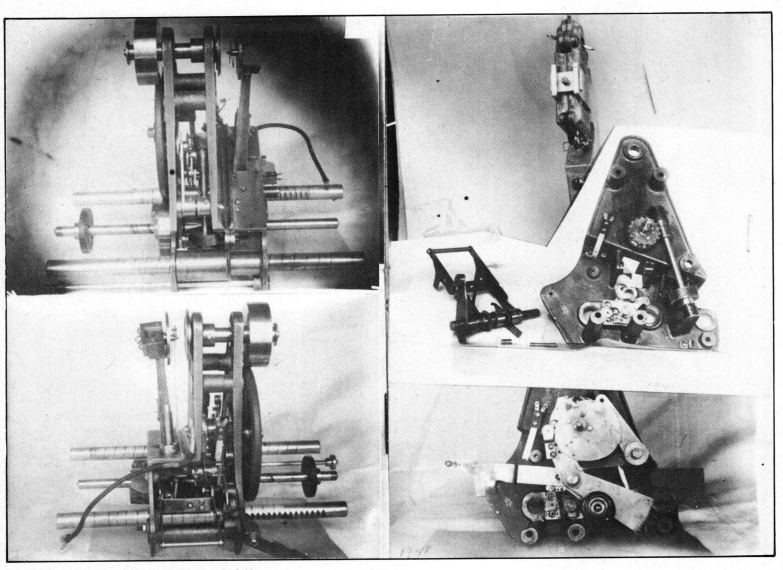

The basic Andrews mechanism of 1941.

Carl McKelvy speaks at a distributors' meeting. The finest general sales manager since Capehart, he masterminded the M100.

The Andrews mechanism after chief engineer Kenney had gone to work on it.

An M100A receiving support from Peggy Lee.

The 'Select-o-matic' 45rpm mechanism used in the M100B gave Seeburg leadership in the industry.

Above: The Seeburg Girls, circa 1949. (Courtesy M. W. Kenney)

Left: M. W. Kenney, Seeburg's chief engineer. (Courtesy M. W. Kenney)

A winning team of executives. Left to right, standing: Mike Hammergren, Carl Johnson, Ray Haimbaugh and Harry King. Seated: Paul Fuller and Roy Waltermade.

Dancing to the juke box in the Deep South. (Courtesy Paul Oliver)

Above: A roadside juke box, used to entertain waiting customers at a drive-in. (Courtesy Paul Oliver)

Right: The model 1422 with 'nuclear sky' lighting effects in a 1946 Rock-Ola brochure. (Courtesy Rock-Ola Manufacturing Corporation)

Rock-Ola 1426, from a brochure illustration. (Courtesy Rock-Ola Manufacturing Corporation)

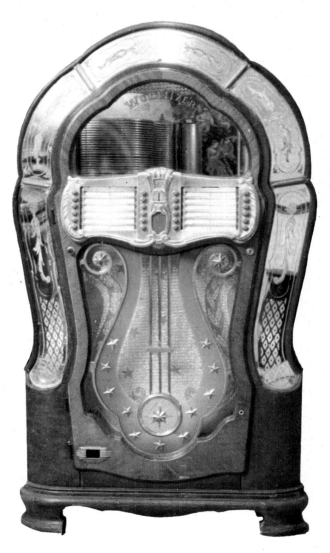

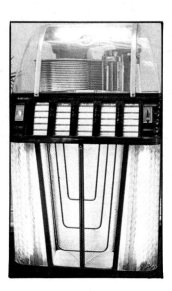

*Above/overleaf: The B17F 'Flying Fortress' bomber was a possible stylistic influence in Paul Fuller's last juke box, the Wurlitzer 1100 of 1948.*

*Left: The 48-selection Rock-Ola 'Rocket', 1950. (Burstein/Krivine)*

7604 Wurlitzer 1080s were shipped in 1946-7. (Courtesy O. Osborn)

*Wurlitzer 1100 of 1948. (Courtesy Sotheby & Co, London)*

# CHAPTER 13

## Mills Novelty Company

IN 1948, when the operators virtually stopped buying new equipment, the newly arrived manufacturers, who had no capital reserves, found themselves in some difficulty. A quite unexpected casualty, however, was the oldest juke box company in the business, Mills Industries.

The company was founded by Herbert Steven Mills. He was born in Iowa in 1870 and moved to Chicago with his family four years later. It is said that his first job was as a newsboy. Herbert was joined by his brothers in the Mills Novelty Company as they entered the field of coin-operated amusement equipment. In 1906 they produced their first music machine, the 'Virtuoso'. 'They sounded poorly but the people played them anyway,

*The Children's Party*

"The reason that boys and girls leave home," once said a keen observer, "is that so few homes are made interesting for young people. The natural craving for amusement very often overcomes personal attachments."

Will you admit that you cannot give your children better reason to pass their evenings with you than to seek elsewhere for an outlet for youthful spirits? If you have sought for means to make your home attractive and have failed to solve the problem, why not get a Violano-Virtuoso? With it you can provide a source of constant interest and enjoyment.

And there is still another important reason why you should have this instrument—it will develop the finer instincts in minds which are most receptive to influence. It will cultivate perceptions and create and enlarge ideals which might otherwise never become matured.

You can buy a piano or a violin, but consider that it will be years before a child can play either of them well, and then only if practice has been a daily duty constantly performed. Why should you spend the money for music lessons, and why should the satisfaction of enjoying the best playing of the best compositions be deferred when you can have a Violano-Virtuoso now?

Look back upon your own childhood and think what it would have meant to you then if you could have had such a means of recreation. Consider how satisfying it would have been for you to learn while still young, all the fine points of musical literature? Do you know them even now?

If you had to sacrifice the advantages given by the Violano-Virtuoso, see that your children have them.

*Advertisement from the* Violano – Virtuoso Handbook, *about 1910.*

because they were so unusual. They were definitely not played for the enjoyment of music' explained Bertie Mills in his interview with Donald Barr.

It consisted of a violin in a cabinet whose strings were played by a revolving disc. Since the motor ran at a constant speed, there was no expression in the music. In 1911, a piano and symetrical harp were added and the machine became the 'Violano Virtuoso'. There were no dealers for this type of equipment in those days, and it was sold directly to the location owners. At that time, Mills was in competition with the J. P. Seeburg and Rudolph Wurlitzer companies for the lucrative player-piano market.

'We had some lawsuits with Wurlitzer [Mills were notorious scrappers and had many legal battles with Wurlitzer]. Nevertheless, Farny would come to the factory and have lunch with my brother, H. S., and so forth. They were friendly enemies; the litigation was over patent infringements and we beat them all the time. They never sued us for anything.'

Herbert was a colourful personality in the industry and is remembered by many for his bizarre sense of humour. Bertie Mills recalls:

'We had a powered house boat. It was about 150 foot long and had a beam of about 30 foot. You could put a lot of people on it; it had two decks. On one occasion, he had guests on the boat and in order to entertain them, he bought out all the tickets to a New York show for an entire week and had the company over on the yacht. He was always full of the devil. Another time, he had about twenty judges to dinner. He had me wire up the table so that underneath the tablecloth I ran a wire to a piece of tin which was underneath each plate and on the sides underneath the forks and knives. When I was given the signal, I would press a button and when they went to pick up their knives and forks, they'd get a shock and throw their knives and forks into the air. Herbert didn't care who it was; he liked to play practical jokes.'

In 1926, Mills Novelty Company brought out their first juke box. It was a large plain wooden cabinet with a viewing window at the top. The records were positioned on a ferris wheel and the machine was fully automatic. It was known as the 'Dance Master'. Bertie Mills recalls the circumstances in 1925:

'My brother [H.S.M.] used to spend six weeks in Florida every year and before he left for Florida in 1925, I said to him, "Herb, there's going to be amplified music now. There are going to be coin-operated phonographs with amplified music. While you're away, I'll make one." He said, "Don't you dare touch or make anything. We're making the 'Violano' and that's it. We don't want any more music." As soon as he left, I started in the experimental room on making one. I had to work like the devil and have it done before he came back, because I knew he would stop us. When he came back, I had the first one playing, and it sounded darn good. It took me several days before I got my brother to go in there and hear it. In the meantime I got fired (not for the first time) because I made it against his wishes, but I would still come down to the factory every day just the same. When he seemed ready to go home, I'd ride with him. I wanted to talk to him and try to show him this thing. I finally got him in there about six o'clock one night. We didn't leave till one o'clock in the morning. We played all the records we had in the place about four times over and he just sat back and listened to them. Next morning when I got to the factory about 9.30, he was already there and down in the tool room where we had the model juke box. He told them to tool up for it. I went in and said, "Herbert, it's not ready for tooling and it's not ready for the market. Let me work on it a couple of months and it will be ready." He said, "Get out of here, I'm doing what I want." He tooled up for it. Thereafter, I had to make a lot of changes and we had to scrap a lot of tools. The first juke box was not selective. It just played the twelve records as they came. Afterwards, I made it selective. The recordings in those days were not uniform. Some played real loud and some were soft. When you put them on a juke box, some would blast out if you had the volume set loud enough to hear the soft ones. So I had a little gadget on the front hub of the machine so that when you put the discs on the machine, you could set the volume for each record so that they would all play at the same volume.'

The Mills Novelty Company never gave the phonograph top priority. They were widely diversified into coin-operated equipment and sold only as many juke boxes as its existing distributor network could handle. One of their best-known products at that time was the 'slot machine', a gambling device which was banned in many of the states but was exported to Europe in large numbers. They had an agent in London who handled this side of the business, which grew considerably in the late 1930s. Fred Mills III, who was a young man at the time, recalls that,

'The Holloway boys used to come to Chicago and my uncles would take them out and show them the town. They used to have a pretty wild

Advertisement in The World's Fair, 1932.

Mills phonograph mechanism, 1940. (Courtesy Automatic Age)

Kay Kyser (minus the Musical Kollege) endorses the Mills 'Empress'. (Automatic Age)

Gabel, a small manufacturer who made quality
phonographs in limited numbers, managed to survive
among the giants. This is the 'Kuro' of 1940.

time. They sent me a sterling silver punch bowl on my wedding – it was engraved "To Mr & Mrs Fred Mills" . . . We all liked the Holloways.'

In 1939, Mills introduced the 'Throne of Music' and the 'Empress', two very popular twenty-selection light-up juke boxes which helped increase Mills's share of the market for that year. They incorporated a new mechanism that had been designed by Smythe, late of Rock-Ola. It was a heavy and slow-moving affair in which the stack of records moved up and down and the selected record was carried out of the stack and placed on to the turntable. It was not a prepossessing sight and the mechanism was not visible to the public.

During the war, Mills was producing armaments for the Government. Bertie Mills explains how one contract came their way:

'The English Government came over to seek out different manufacturers to make things for them, ammunition and so forth, and they wanted bomb releases manufactured and we were recommended. Well, the people from England thought that it was ridiculous to go to a novelty company to build bomb releases. They flew to Chicago and we met them at the factory on a Sunday. They saw the plant and the type of equipment we had and knew that there was no question about our ability to make what they wanted.'

Mills had a reputation in the industry for the quality of their products. As Bertie puts it:

'We had an excellent factory; we were integrated manufacturers. We did everything ourselves and didn't have to job out anything. We designed and made our own tools, did our own woodwork and metalwork. We had the best craftsmen and weren't afraid to take on any job.'

In 1944, Herbert S. Mills, the founder of the firm, died and his brother Bertie retired; much of the running of the business fell into the hands of the managers and the name of the company was changed to Mills Industries.

The post-war juke box was called the 'Constellation'. In addition to the modern aluminium cabinet it incorporated a brand new mechanism, very similar to the AMI record changer. Despite the tremendous demand for phonographs at this time, the 'Constellation' was not a popular machine. All the other manufacturers had continued with their old mechanisms and concentrated on new cabinet styles. They saw no need to redesign the record changer when the market was willing to accept the original one, and in any case, it normally takes at least two years to design, model, test and develop a new system. Mills were taking a big risk for no apparent reason. In the event, the new mechanism did prove unsatisfactory in the first months and many phonographs were being returned to the factory; Mills had to redesign and make very expensive adjustments to the equipment. In addition, contrary to their normal practice, they had sub-contracted the cabinets to Bell Aircraft and the 13,000 cabinets they had ordered were more than they could use.

They also brought out the 'Panorama'. It was a video juke box but they had problems with the film. Jimmy Roosevelt (the President's son) was making the cassettes for them but they were too expensive for the operators and the machine died for lack of a product.

Before the war, Mills had won an important contract from the Coca-Cola company to build bottle dispensers. Following the same misguided policy, they dropped the reliable and adequate pre-war model and made a new vending machine for 1946. Again they didn't test it for long enough before it went into production, and Coca-Cola returned them all and cancelled the contract.

The slot machine business was down to nothing because of laws that prohibited the shipment of machines or parts across state lines, and the war had deprived them of the expanding overseas market. They had lost their staple product; these blows, combined with the minor recession of the late 1940s, placed the organisation in serious difficulties. Fred Mills explains:

'We were forced into chapter eleven bankruptcy and lost propriety of the products and the patents. We had to shrink everything down to liquidate. The guy who was brought in to do the job was ruthless, he just got rid of everything. We got about $50,000 for everything, the huge factory premises, all that fine equipment. The people who bought it stripped it down and made about $2,000,000. In 1941, the business had been valued at $10,000,000. It was a great shame, a great loss.'

*Mills 'Throne of Music'. (Acme Attractions)*

*Mills 'Empress', 1939. (Acme Attractions)*

# CHAPTER 14
## Speed Test

IN 1944, Columbia Broadcasting had begun the search for a practical slow-speed micro-groove record. Their objective was to produce a record that would play classical compositions for up to half an hour without the accustomed breaks for turning over the record. By1948, this had been achieved and Columbia presented their 33⅓rpm long-playing record. They had a formidable task in front of them. The entire industry was geared to 78rpm discs and had developed an inborn resistance to change. But the LP had a few other things in its favour; it was made out of a light unbreakable plastic; in reducing the weight of the tone arm to suit the new microgroove, they had substantially improved the quality of the sound, and it was a novelty. Columbia marketed a record player for the new discs and a massive promotional campaign was set in motion. By 1949, some 1,250,000 copies at 33⅓rpm had been sold.

RCA had been caught unawares by Columbia's coup, and maintained a stoic silence about the whole affair. But they had no intention of allowing Columbia to steal a march on them. Half-way through 1949, RCA came out with their own version of the microgroove, smaller at 7in diameter and a little faster at 45rpm. They naturally produced their own record player which retailed for $12.95 and initiated their own promotional programme. There was no rational reason why RCA should want a speed of their own and people still say to this day that they did the industry a lot of harm in doing what they did.

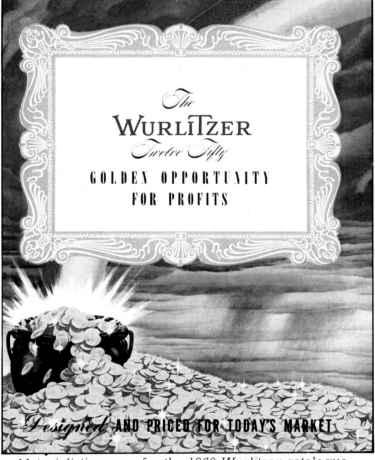

*Materialistic cover for the 1950 Wurlitzer catalogue.*

The 78 was finished, that much was clear. But the public was very confused about which records and record players to buy. Many decided to wait and see, and this was reflected in the fall-off in total record sales from 204,000,000 in 1947 to 153,000,000 in 1949. But Columbia were gaining ground and by 1950 almost all the other record companies had gone over to 33⅓. In January of that year RCA finally capitulated and announced they too would be offering records at 33⅓rpm; at that time, several top executives who were held responsible by the shareholders for the disasterous policy were dismissed. But the company decided to persevere with the 45 and in 1950 alone spent $5,000,000 in publicity for this product. They still maintained that the 45 was the more suitable for popular recordings and could co-exist peacefully with the LP which was, after all, for more serious music. In this belief they were supported by one of the most powerful figures in the music industry, Carl T. McKelvy, general sales manager of Seeburg.

As soon as RCA had presented their 7in disc, McKelvy knew at once that it was ideally suited for juke box operations. It was light, unbreakable and small. It was preferable even to the 33⅓rpm LP not only because it was smaller, but because it played faster. From the operators' standpoint, the faster it played, the shorter the playing time for each record. Therefore more money could be taken every hour; McKelvy always kept the operators in mind. In addition to this, he knew

Model 4007 Oval DeLuxe Speaker

Model 4005-A Round Walnut Speaker

Model 4009 Recessed Wall or Ceiling Speaker

Model 4000 Silver Star Wall or Ceiling Speaker

*The full range of wall speakers available from Wurlitzer in 1950.*

The 1950 catalogue featured the model 1250, a 48-selection juke box available for either 78, 45 or 33⅓ rpm operation. 13,496 were shipped.

Model 1450

*Wurlitzer model 1450. 4085 were shipped between 1951 and 1953.*

Model 1500

*The Wurlitzer 1500.*

that the Andrews mechanism could adapt quickly and inexpensively to the new record. He wrote to his operators:

'If and when the 45rpm record is generally accepted by the public and its many advantages become desirable in the coin-operated phonograph business, their 78rpm "Select-O-Matic" mechanisms will be exchanged for 45rpm mechanisms at nominal cost.'

Thus Seeburg, having recently taken over the leadership of an industry that accounted for a large proportion of total record sales, had thrown its weight firmly behind RCA's gamble and played a major role in its ultimate success. The other record companies gradually moved over to 45rpm for their popular recordings (including Columbia) and in 1954, 200,000,000 45s were sold.

Seeburg came out with the M100B in 1950, the first exclusively 45rpm juke box, and actually supplied operators with the records if they were unable to obtain the records themselves. Parkoff recalls that:

'We felt that the whole industry would go to the small record. The initiative came from Seeburg. They put their money on the line to produce the 45rpm when they were just a small segment of the record industry. They said the future of the record industry would be in vinyl records. The M100B was the biggest juke box I ever had. I sold 2000 in my territory alone [New York].'

The other manufacturers were still not convinced. They must have been hoping that the 45rpm promotional drive would not succeed and that Seeburg would, as a result, be up the creek without a paddle. In 1950-2, Rock-Ola, Wurlitzer

and AMI hedged their bets, and each model was offered with an optional conversion kit to 45 and 33⅓rpm. They did not make the decision to go into 45rpm until 1953.

But their problem was twofold. Not only did they have to change the speed and size of the record changer, but, if they were to keep up with Seeburg, they had to increase the number of selections. The stack of records that had been such an asset in the 1940s was now a major liability. The stack could not be increased without making the mechanism unduly complicated and a new system would take at least two years to develop. So they resorted to intermediate solutions.

Rock-Ola's 'Rocket' of 1950 played the record on both sides by giving the tone arm two styli, one above and one below; when the lower side of the record was selected (odd numbers), the record was pulled out of the stack in the normal way but the motor was reversed. When the disc was in position, the spring-loaded tone arm played the lower side. In this way, Rock-Ola's selection capability was doubled, although it was a machine that required constant adjustment.

Wurlitzer did much the same, and in 1952 made the extraordinary decision to add an extra twenty-six stack on the other side of the tone arm. Apart from making the mechanism rather complicated, the juke box had to be considerably enlarged to accomodate the new system; this was the heaviest juke box ever built. Although they had succeeded in producing a 104-play phonograph without substantially changing the

*Rock-Ola model 1432, 1950. (Courtesy Rock-Ola Manufacturing Corporation)*

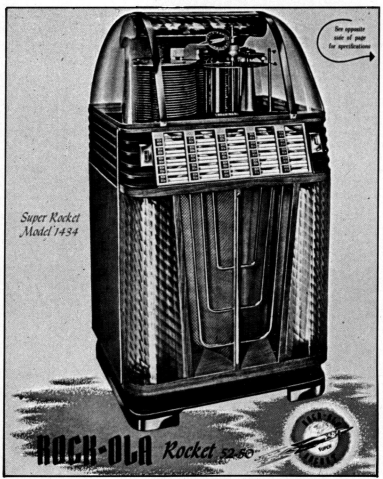

*Rock-Ola 'Rocket', 1950-2. (Courtesy Rock-Ola Manufacturing Corporation)*

Rock-Ola 'Fireball', 1952. (Courtesy Rock-Ola Manufacturing Corporation)

Rock-Ola 'Comet', 1953. (Courtesy Rock-Ola Manufacturing Corporation)

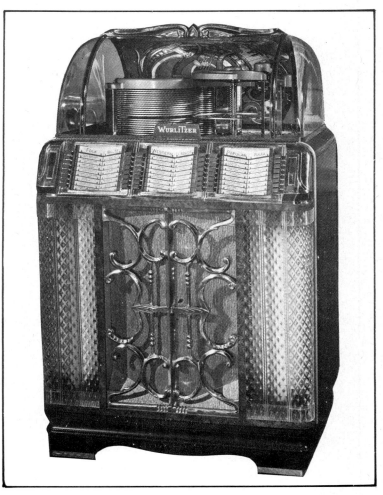

The 48-selection Wurlitzer 1400, available for 78, 45 or 33⅓rpm operation. 14,304 shipped.

mechanism, it was not a successful machine and only 8383 were manufactured.

While Seeburg's main competitors ponderously came round to their way of thinking, several new companies entered the field. Ristaucrat Inc came out with a twelve-play 45rpm miniature juke box. Williams, the pinball people, began shipping their 'Music Mite' in 1951 and another pinball manufacturer, Chicago Coin, produced their own 45rpm phonograph, the 'Hit Parade'. H. C. Evans was now making a 40-selection job with plans for a 100-selection juke box in the pipeline, but in the event all these four manufacturers left the industry within two years of having started.

In 1952, Rock-Ola produced an adequate competitor to the Seeburg 'Select-O-Matic'. It had a carousel mechanism that could accomodate 120 records of any size. The 'Fireball' model of that year was a good seller for Rock-Ola and helped them regain a share of the market. By 1953, it was clear that 45rpm records were here to stay, and the company brought out their first exclusively 45rpm juke box.

After the Model 1500 disaster of 1952, Wurlitzer speeded up the development of a successor to the Wurlitzer stack which had served them for 18 years. A. D. Palmer had replaced Mike Hammergren as general sales manager and had been gradually rebuilding the Wurlitzer distributor organisation. Joe Clement, who had worked with Paul Fuller, and had been a great admirer of the man, was now Wurlitzer's chief stylist, while Fred H. Osborne, in charge of the engineering department, was making up for lost time; in 1953 he had designed a carousel-type mechanism, not unlike Rock-Ola's, which offered 104 selections.

While Rock-Ola and Seeburg had been equivocating over the question of quantity and speed,

AMI were steadily increasing their share of the market. They had abandoned their unique distributor/operator network just before the start of World War Two and were offering their post-war models to independent operators for the first time. Their record changer, despite being the oldest in the industry, was still one of the best designed, and made the transition to 45rpm effortlessly.

By 1952, there were 35,000 45rpm juke boxes in operation throughout America. Seeburg had entered into an agreement with RCA that enabled them to guarantee their operators the widest possible range of recordings for their equipment. By 1954, it was estimated that over 70% of all new equipment on the market had been manufactured by Seeburg.

The question of a nickel or a dime per play had been hotly debated by the industry since the end of the war. The manufacturers were inclined towards the latter, because they felt that the increased earnings would result in larger orders for new equipment. The operators were worried that the elasticity of demand would be sufficient to wipe out any advantage gained by the higher price, especially in the poorer locations. There was always the danger that the dime operator would be undercut by the nickel operator. The newly formed MOA (Music Operators of America) addressed itself to this problem in 1950 and began working on a formula for making the change (by now a little overdue) and enforcing it; it would also require the understanding of the location owners. They were assisted in this matter by the decision of the New York Telephone Company to change from nickels to dimes as the basic unit of payment. In 1950, it was argued, coffee cost a dime. The last juke box that would accept the 5 cent coin was manufactured in 1951.

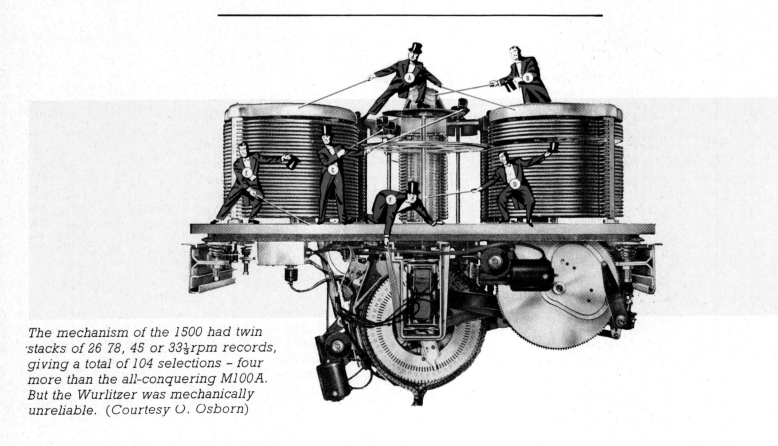

*The mechanism of the 1500 had twin stacks of 26 78, 45 or 33⅓rpm records, giving a total of 104 selections – four more than the all-conquering M100A. But the Wurlitzer was mechanically unreliable. (Courtesy O. Osborn)*

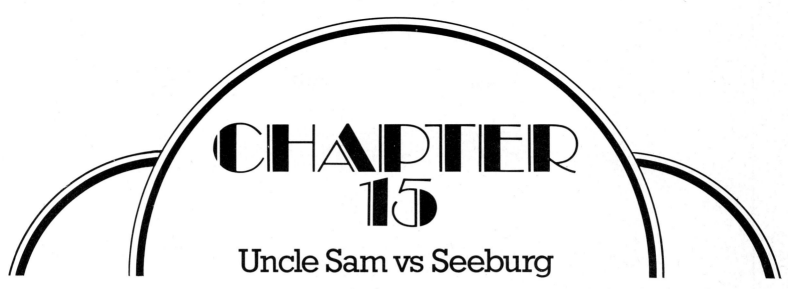

# CHAPTER 15

## Uncle Sam vs Seeburg

URING THE mid-1950s, the United States Justice Department was examining the distributorship arrangements that operated within certain manufacturing industries. When it came to the phonograph industry, the investigating committee selected Seeburg, and initiated legal proceedings under the Sherman Anti-Trust Act. N. Marshall Seeburg II recalls the circumstances.

*Seeburg:* 'We had a system for keeping track of all the serial numbers. If a foreign machine showed up which had a Florida number, we could say, ''What the hell

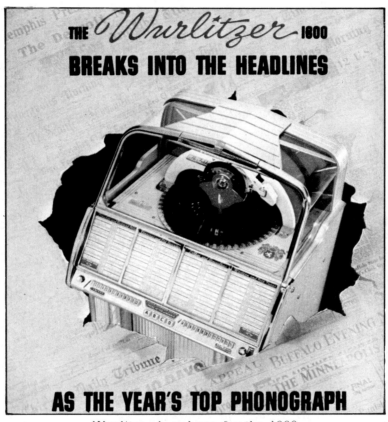

*Wurlitzer brochure for the 1800.*

is it doing in Milwaukee?'' If the excuse was lame, our franchise was cancellable on ninety days notice. The other people had analogous arrangements. If we learned that there was wholesale piracy of territory, we would cancel it. We policed our own distributorship organisation. It was a valuable franchise and we had to keep it that way by stopping people raiding other people's territory. It didn't happen often, because we were careful in selecting our distributors in the first place.

'We were tagged by Uncle Sam as the leader of the industry. The Justice Department found us criminally in violation of the Sherman Anti-Trust Act. We were accused of imposing ''unreasonable restraints on channels.'' The theory of the law is, if I sell something to you, I retain no rights over it. Our attempt to hand out exclusive territory was in violation of the law.

'It was great in legal theory, but a disaster in practice. You can never tell what animates the Government.'

*Krivine:* 'What do you think it was?'

*Seeburg:* 'I don't really know. Maybe it was a distributor who had more influence than we realised. It might have been the hoods. It was a time when exclusive distributorships were being attacked in many industries. As a matter of fact, there was a case against Philco who had a very similar distributorship to ours, and they had an identical action. The idea was that Philco would expend all their time and energy taking the matter to the Supreme Court. Unfortunately, Philco took a Consent Decree, i.e. ''Tell us what we're not supposed to do and we won't do it any more''; you go before the Judge, he gives you a twenty page document, and tells you to sign here. Now we were next in the firing line. With the prospect of five years of litigation ahead of us, we said: ''If it's good enough for Philco, it's good enough for us.'' So we took a Consent Decree. As a result, we had to destroy all our serial number records, and we lost control of our distributor organisation. This was to the detriment of the industry. The franchise was debased, not worth so much. Undesirable elements could wheel and deal with your products in ways they hadn't been able to before.

'This was one of the reasons we decided to quit the business. At the time we had 80% of the market, and although our equipment was the most expensive we were very profitable. The profit on each machine was better than 30%. It was obvious that unions were coming; we had always bent over backwards to maintain good relations with our work force, and the idea of a union operation was distasteful – we knew we would lose control over our factory.

'Secondly, the overseas market was drying up. Our dealers had developed a system of trade-ins, refurbishing and then shipping them overseas. The dealers called it "flushing the toilet". We also did well in supplying the parts to the overseas machines. Now Europe was recovering, they would start making their own equipment, and we would no longer be able to maintain our high production.

'Thirdly, to stay alive on a capital basis, you had to diversify – horizontally into vending, or into a new industry. That was a capital risk that my father did not want to take.

'What really decided it was something of a personal nature. We had a bereavement in the family, and my father lost his taste for the business. He knew that when he died, we would lose control of it. The family owned all the stock, and because the business was such a valuable asset, we would have to sell stock to pay the Estate Tax. My brother and I weren't so interested in the business; I'm not a manufacturer by temperament or by training. I'm a financial man by necessity. It was my best judgement in 1956 that we should quit while we were ahead.' [N.M.S. sold the assets for more than $10,000,000].

*Krivine:* 'Did you keep track of the business after that?'

*Seeburg:* 'When I walked out of the factory, that was the last I ever thought about it – until the cheque cleared.'

*Old men in diner, Indiana, by Peter Stackpole. (Time-Life Picture Agency)*

# CHAPTER 16

## King of the Title Strips

IN THE early 1930s Dick Steinberg was a 'coin' man operating on the northeastern seaboard of the USA. His experience since then has extended into many aspects of the industry and he is now one of the most respected of all members of the juke box operating fraternity. Even today he is built like a football player and talks with a heavy New Jersey accent.

'I was with Federal Steel in Newark, a small metal manufacturer which made cigar boxes for vending machines called "Peggy O'Neals" The cigars sold for five cents although there were no real coin mechanisms in those days. I worked on a 5% commission. I sold seventy-five per cent of the output. In 1934 I bought my first La Salle. Everywhere business was bad. I did O.K. Federal Steel tried to cut my commission, so I went out on my own. I teamed up with two partners, they were brothers, you know, and we bought a few counter games from Howard Peo in Rochester. We had machines in speakeasies which were in basements of homes, backs of shops, garages and above stores, as well as restaurants and hotels. I always gave them an extra machine in case it broke down. If there was a bust, I'd lose a machine, what did it cost in those days . . . $23? Anyway, there was no identification.

'You ask me what makes a good operator? We had a former prohibition agent. They busted him for some things he did wrong. He knew everything, where everything was all through the countryside. Stewart S. Stone was his name, with a dollar mark through the S. [Laughs] He was an alcoholic. I used to bail him out of jail every three

*The Seeburg 100W of 1953. It sold for $1050.*
*(Courtesy K. Baxter)*

months. Finally, I said to him, Stoney . . . he had a terrific mouthpiece, terrific gall, you know. He'd go out even in the city of New York. He'd throw his hat into the corner, right there, pointing . . . he'd say . . . "See, see there where my hat is. I guarantee you fifty dollars a month for that space." "How?" they asked. "We'll put in one of our licensed games." "Put it in," they said. The truck would follow him up and install them. They weren't getting fifty dollars a month, they were getting a hundred dollars a month. Sometimes he would place as many as twenty, twenty-five a day.

'In 1932, I used to drive around in my La Salle. We had 1200 locations from Point Pleasant, New Jersey to the Delaware Water Gap. On Monday morning I'd get into the Caddy and I'd pick up dough from one point to the next and come back with, well . . . a lot of money. I'd be doing fifty stops a day. That's called a run.

'I didn't mind running around with all that money in the trunk; after all, who knew it? I didn't advertise it. [Pause] I couldn't get insurance in the thirties, and I knew the principal of a big insurance firm in Newark. They wouldn't give me life insurance. [Laughs] That's what the business was like in those days. During the Depression I always had ten thousand dollars on the street, people I'd paid to take my machines. I gave a lot of people credit. We helped the catering industry. I had a friend, a lawyer, who wasn't getting much work at the time. I put him on a retainer, I didn't need a lawyer, I could look after myself. But anyway I gave him two hundred dollars a month.

Four male Seeburgs. (Courtesy K. Baxter)

JUSTUS P. SEEBURG II (BUZZ) (GRANDSON)
JUSTUS P. SEEBURG I (GRANDFATHER)
MARSHALL N. SEEBURG (SON OF J.P. SEEBURG I)
NOEL M. SEEBURG (GRANDSON) LAWYER

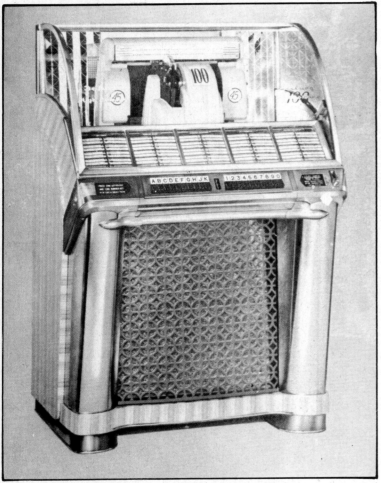

The Seeburg HF100R, from a publicity shot.

Seeburg
KD200. 1956.
(Courtesy
K. Baxter)

In 1935, I got involved in manufacturing electrical components for ski-ball alleys. It failed; I remember it cost me eighty-five thousand dollars. That's how much I'd made after a few years as an operator. They cleaned me out. I sold my radio rifles, my automatic baseball games. They had the chapter eleven. I was down. My lawyer asked me how much I needed to get started. He sat down and wrote me out a cheque for five thousand dollars. There was no problem making money in that business. Some of the guys just didn't know how to keep it.

'The first juke box I bought was in 1934. A P10. Wurlitzer was the king pin of the business. He had a merchandising genius in Capehart. He sold me two carloads of phonographs. All he expected me to do was pay the freight. Everything was paper. I could have had ten carloads. If I didn't want to pay the freight, he would have prepaid it for me. He didn't even know me; he knew of me. Later, we got acquainted. Each car could hold forty phonographs. The P10 cost two hundred and thirty-nine dollars. It was a massive piece of furniture, built for the ages.

'Most of my phonographs were Wurlitzers. The 750E was the greatest juke box ever built. It looked right and it took a lot of money. I remember I bought a mess of "Singing Towers". It was a disaster. I couldn't get them to work. The guy I sold them to made a lot of money out of them because the war was on. I had a few "Hi Tones" too, and they were good machines . .

'In 1942, I volunteered for the Army. I was in England, you know, a fine country. When I came back to New Jersey in '45, I didn't go back to operating. While I had been away, I got to thinking about the music programming side of the business.

'In those days, you had four record companies, Columbia, RCA Victor, Capitol and Decca. There were no independent record distributors; you had to drive to each company outlet to get all the records you needed for your machines. I remember when Jack Kapp started Decca in '34, I was paying 19c for Bing Crosby. The salesman would come over and give you the razzmatazz, snapping his fingers, this is great, but on the juke box it didn't make a dime. You had to buy them in boxes of 25 and you didn't really know what you were buying. It was all guesswork, and if you guessed wrong, you had to sell the records off at 10c. That's the way we used to do it. So I started a service to help the operators. I had a news-sheet printed out with information about which records were coming up. I sent it off to the operators and they would then ask for the title strips. It's got to be fast, the operators have to know which records are coming up because that's the time when they get the maximum play; once they are up and they can be heard on the radio, they're no good to the juke box. That's the way it works. We are the fastest printers in the world. They call at 3pm and ask for a record that no one's ever heard of and the title strip is in the post by 4pm. A record will sell 40,000 titles before

Wurlitzer 2300 'Stereophonic'. (Courtesy M. Trussell)

120-selection Rock-Ola 1454. (Courtesy Rock-Ola Manufacturing Corporation)

Rock-Ola 1448, 1955. (Courtesy Rock-Ola Manufacturing Corporation)

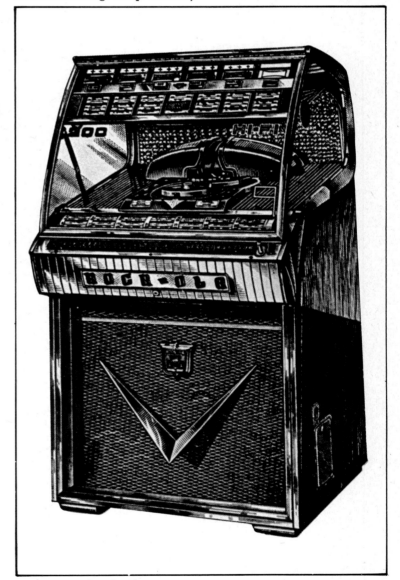

Rock-Ola 1457. (Courtesy Rock-Ola Manufacturing Corporation)

it's even in the shops, it's what's called initial action. The named artist is the most powerful thing in the business, when he's hot. When the 100-selection boxes came in, I developed a colour code for the titles. Red for popular; orange, easy listening; green, country; blue, soul; magenta, oldies or standards; brown for latin or chicano. Not everyone went for my idea. I seem to recall that I locked horns with McKelvy [Seeburg], he wouldn't have it; I had two words for that guy. The colour code helped people find the record they wanted. I used to tell my customers that it could increase their earnings by three dollars a week on each machine. I fought hard for the colour system and eventually educated the country on it. I sold the magazine and now I do just the strips. I supply them to one-stops throughout the United States.

'After the war, a few enterprising people like Herb Cohen and his brother who had worked for RCA became independent record distributors. They bought records from all the companies and sold them to the operators. [Harry Brockman of Uptown Music, St Louis, advertised, "Stop running around in circles, we ship all labels within 24 hours and 5c over regular wholesale."] The operators could buy all the records they needed – and as few – in one stop. That's how we came to call them one-stops. The distributors were glad to get rid of the operators, they thought they were a cut above, they preferred to do business with the record shops.

'When 200-selection juke boxes were introduced, music programming became much more of a science [by 1957, 60% of all operators in America were buying at one-stops] and the operators really need the service. I can tell by the number of title strips they take what business the one-stops are doing. Philadelphia has a quarter of the population, the news that it sells three times the title strips of the New York market leads me to say that New York doesn't buy records and doesn't have the income of the Philadelphia operators. You figure, 10% of the income is used for record replacement and in Philly, five to eight records are rotated each week. New York would be lucky if it could manage eight records per month.'

Joseph Clement-styled Wurlitzer 2500 of 1960-2. (Courtesy M. Trussell)

Wurlitzer 2200 of 1958, with Johnny Ray. 4315 were sold. (Courtesy M. Trussell)

Rock-Ola 'Tempo II', 1959.

# CHAPTER 17

## Operating (Where's the Mob?)

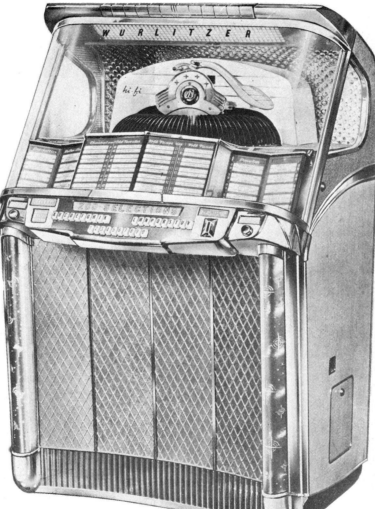

*200-selection Wurlitzer 2100. 4347 were sold between 1956 and 1958. (Courtesy M. Trussell)*

ALTHOUGH THERE is nothing intrinsically disreputable about juke boxes, they are very vulnerable to undesirable elements in the operating business. Operating is a strictly cash business; the agreements between operator and location owner are usually of a verbal nature and the equipment is located in taverns and clubs which are, after all, the places where bad people go . . .

'We entertain the public by giving them the opportunity of playing music while having a drink. We are the poor man's entertainment business. Some people seem to think that operating is easy money but it isn't. It's hard work, it's getting a location, placing equipment in the location and seeing to it that's it's serviced properly when it breaks down. Weekly collections, changing of records, keeping the machine clean and giving the public what it wants in the way of musical selection. Machines do break down and they have to be repaired immediately, not next week, because being an income-producing piece of equipment, if you leave it out of order for a few days there is a loss of revenue for the operator. He can't afford a loss of revenue, he must repair that piece of equipment quickly. In addition to that, the location owner wants that machine available at all times and if it is out of order his customers complain that they are not being entertained when they buy a drink, and he can't afford that because it is a supplemental part of his business.'

(Meyer Parkoff, interviewed in 1975)

'There are all sorts of guys in the operating business. Some of them aren't so smart. Humbert Betty Sr of North Bergen, New Jersey, had a name for them. He called them "coolies". They did everything on their own. They made a living for their family by their own sweat. They didn't hire anybody otherwise they wouldn't have a paycheck for themselves. They didn't rotate their machines, they didn't buy them right. They gave too much away to the location owner. They didn't have reserves.'

(Dick Steinberg)

The juke box industry had a monkey on its back since the days of prohibition. When you say coin machines, you think of slots. When you say slots, you think of racketeers. This was, to a large extent, true before 1933, but when repeal came, the speakeasies disappeared and the juke box locations came into the ownership of legitimate businessmen. When Wurlitzer started manufacturing in 1934, Capehart endeavoured to give the operators a sense of identity and a sense of pride as a means of stabilising the industry and strengthening his market. He organised conventions and outings, and membership of the prestigious Century Club was the goal of all operators. In 1939, Capehart planned a cruise for a thousand operators on the luxury French liner *Île de France*. He wrote pamphlets and made speeches, urging them 'to raise their status from mere coin opera-

*Georgie Shaw listens to his hit recording 'There Must Be Some Mistake' on a 104-selection, 45rpm Wurlitzer 1700.*

*Artist's impression of a 1955 Seeburg juke box. (Courtesy M. W. Kenney)*

tors to that of music merchants.'

The operating industry has constantly been the subject of 'yellow journalism' and the relationship between the press and the coin machine has been far from happy as this interview conducted by Donald Barr with Bert Mills of the Mills Novelty Company, amply illustrates.

*Barr:* 'Mr Mills, *Fortune* magazine's November 1932 issue contains an article entitled, ''Plums, Cherries and Murder.'' Do you remember that article?'

*Mills:* 'Yes, I remember it. The reporter whc wrote the article came to me to ask all about the percentages on the reel machines. I made up all of the percentages from the very beginning. They had a phony story on the reels and asked me to help them correct it. I helped them out, but they didn't publish it the way I told it to them. It was erroneous.'

*Barr:* 'Rumour has it that Fred, who at that time was the President of the Company, believed that the Company was going to get a million dollars worth of good publicity out of the article. Is that true?'

*Mills:* 'That whole article backfired and he [Fred] said and swore up and down that he would never let another reporter in that Company. You see, they twisted the story. They took stuff out of context and said that we said it. Like most reporters, they wanted to build up the story, and so they changed it to suit themselves.'

Operators have often been accused of submitting false tax returns. This is doubtless quite true because juke boxes don't accept cheques and under these circumstances, you would have to be an extremely good citizen to resist the temptation to make one or two minor adjustments. But operators didn't have it all their own way as this extract from an emotionally charged article by Ralph Young (*circa* 1935) suggests. He instances

'Persecution, unjust and discriminatory taxation tantamount to virtual confiscation as a result of untruthful statements by manufacturers as to earnings, that were widely circulated and used against us as authoritative statements by executives in the industry . . . and so on endlessly.'

The operators formed themselves into local associations for the dual purpose of protecting their interests within the industry, and improving their image to the community as a whole.

'We did a missionary job for the manufacturer. I opened up Bergen County [New Jersey]; the local governor had imposed penal taxes on machines in order to keep them out. We sent letters signed by different people, put ads in the local papers and were lobbying constantly.'

(Dick Steinberg)

If an outsider came into an area and tried to undercut the competition by giving the location owners better commission deals, or offering the public two plays for a nickel, the association could put pressure on the distributor to stop supplying the man with new equipment. They could protect themselves against the distributor/operator, an institution that was, in those days, a bit below the belt. The local associations were also a means of keeping out the undesirables.

In 1948, the operating fraternity was faced with a much more serious problem. During the war, Petrillo's powerful Musician's Union had succeeded in putting the screws on the record industry by extracting, for the first time, a modest royalty on each record sold. Now they turned their attention to the juke box. The success of this machine in the restaurants and taverns of America had been directly at the expense of performing musicians and they were demanding compensation. Whereas in 1942, Petrillo had achieved his objectives by industrial action, the battle with the juke box industry was to be a legislative one.

The musicians were demanding a 'tax' to be levied on every phonograph located in public places. The effect of such a move would be to knock out thousands of marginal operators and cut into the profits of the rest. Sixty-eight officers of state groups met in Chicago in 1948 and hastily convened the Music Operators of America in order to meet this challenge. The so-called Scott-Fellows juke box bills went through Congress three times during the next two years and were defeated each time by the MOA lobby. The American Society of Composers, Authors and Publishers tried again in 1951 with the more detailed Bryson Bill and this was killed in the House Judiciary Committee, as was the McCarran Bill of 1953 and the O'Mahoney Bill of 1956. The MOA had started out as an *ad hoc* fourteen-man committee under the chairmanship of the intrepid George Miller. In 1952 he was elected President, and the MOA was officially incorporated. Miller's vision was of an organisation embracing the entire music industry, including the composers, the record companies, the juke box operators and the phonograph manufacturers within which framework all differences could be discussed in a democratic manner and resolved without recourse to the law. But he was frustrated by the lack of support from his own operators and the recalcitrance of the big five manufacturers, and the MOA never developed beyond a loose federation of strong regional associations during our period.

We have noted that the music operators encountered some difficulties in the field of public relations. That is to say, there are those who have suggested that the jukebox business is heavily populated by elements who conduct their affairs in an un-American way. The question that all students of coin machines love to ask is, 'Where's the Mob?'

An article appeared in *The World's Fair* (the British entertainment trade journal) on 11 October 1958, headed, 'Those Americans leave me breathless.' Bingo Beaufort reports that:

'During the week I spent in New York and

*Diner with Seeburg wall boxes (behind ketchup)*

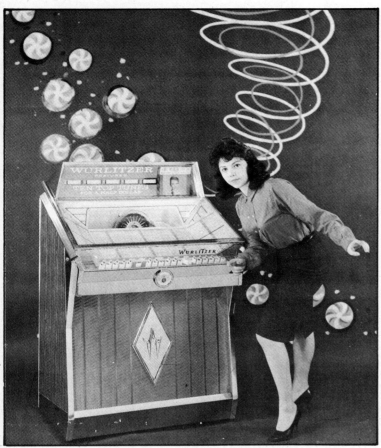

*Twisting to one of the 3372 Wurlitzer 2600s shipped in 1961-2.*

Chicago, I was able to visit many of the top manufacturers and jobbers and to talk to some of the leading personalities in the business there. Personalities did I say? Great-hearted human dynamos would be nearer the mark. They're terrific. Ruthless perhaps. Sharp as needles, for sure. Tireless too. Always on the job and on the ball. Rude, crude and harsh sometimes, but lovable withall. And more American than the Stars and Stripes . . .

'Most [of the executives] I met start their day at 8.30am and don't much mind how long they work. As far as they are concerned the coin machine industry is a devoted life. That is certainly the way to keep an industry fresh and lively.

An English operator was in America in 1970 on business and was visiting the offices of an East Coast distributor who had been supplying him with equipment.

'Half way through our discussions, he received a phone call that lasted no more than a few minutes. He became very agitated and the colour seemed to drain from his face. When he put the phone down, he was visibly shaken. I pretended not to notice but he went ahead and told me what it was about. Apparently one of his salesmen had

*Catalogue picture of the 2600 in location.*

accidentally crossed over into an adjacent territory and the distributor in that territory, who had been informed about the infringement, had called up my friend to express himself on the matter. What in England would have been regarded as a simple misunderstanding, over there seemed to be a matter of life and death.'

These two observers were struck by the intensity of American business. It is an environment in which the market forces are allowed to operate freely with the inevitable result that commerce is highly competitive. It is also a society in which commercial considerations come before all else, and under these circumstances, businessmen establish their own set of rules and their own standards of behaviour in their dealings with one another. On this level, the juke box business is no different to any other business in America.

Consider next a scenario which has been created to illustrate a second category.

Two men walk into an empty tavern in San Antone, Texas on a warm afternoon. One man stands at the bar and speaks to the barman. 'How come your man hasn't been to repair your juke box?' The barman, taken aback by this unexpected question, begins to explain that there is nothing wrong with the juke box, but is interrupted by a heavy crash as the juke box is tipped over on to its fragile fascia by the second man. He then lifts the juke box back into the upright position, and the first visitor says to the barman, 'Well, there is now. But you're lucky I happened to be passing because I operate a route in these parts and I do believe that I have a very good piccolo in my truck there. Now, I might be persuaded to locate my piece of equipment in your tavern and I can give you a firm guarantee that my juke box won't break down in the way this old one did.' Meanwhile, the second man has wheeled in the new phonograph and the transaction has been completed. It only remains for the barman to call up the dispossessed operator to ask him – without going into details – to remove his equipment.

When confronted by the Arturo Ui school of business administration, the little man is virtually helpless. The law enforcement agencies can only help him (if indeed they are willing) if the barman (or any other witness) is prepared to make a statement, and if the latter is of a nervous disposition, this might not be forthcoming. The injured party will probably not be able to sue the tavern for 'breach of contract' or even 'malicious damage' because most agreements of this nature are verbal understandings.

He attempts to lobby the local mayor with a view to having the interloper's licence revoked, but it then becomes a political matter and the good mayor will have to take into account the proximity of the next elections and the fact that the gentleman who recently bumped into a juke box is married to his wife's cousin.

The operator then calls on the local distributors to warn them that there is a gangster operating in their territories and that they should stop supplying him with equipment. The distributor

Senator Capehart, meanwhile, was moving in higher circles in D.C.

Rock-Ola 'Princess', 1961. (Courtesy Rock-Ola Manufacturing Corporation)

Rock-Ola 'Music Vendor', 1958. (Courtesy Rock-Ola Manufacturing Corporation)

then has to consider his own position and eventually decides that a more aggressive type of operator is exactly what the territory needs, and he is very sorry that he can't be more helpful.

But our operator doesn't give up so easily; he writes a letter to the all-powerful general sales manager of the manufacturing company he deals with, appealing for help. The general sales manager takes out the file on the distributor for the area in question, and notes that he has one of the best sales figures in the country and that he seems to be running his outfit efficiently. He writes back to the operator in San Antone, advising him to contact the local police without delay. (It is worth noting that even if the general sales manager had decided to take up our operator's case and had wished, therefore, to discipline the negligent distributor, he would have been powerless to do so after the 1956 anti-trust action.)

How probable are the events described? There are certain areas in America, notably sections of Chicago, Detroit and New York, where it is difficult to run any business legitimately. Bakeries, linen hire, cab companies, radio stations and even the town hall might all, to some extent, be controlled by a cartel of crime, and in such an environment, the juke box is easy prey. On the other hand, the great majority of communities in America offer no opportunity for the criminal talent and they will have no difficulty in getting rid of undesirables. In areas which are neither all good nor all bad, the existence of a strong Operators Association can tip the balance in favour of the little man.

The third category concerns the mythical entity known to the American public as 'Mr Juke Box'.

Let us consider the rock 'n' roll epic by 20th Century Fox, *The Girl Can't Help It*.

It is the story of an ex-convict, Fats Murdock ('they used to call me "Slim"') who falls in love with shapely Jerry Jordan (played convincingly by Jayne Mansfield). But because he is a big shot, he's got to make her into a star (he can't marry an 'unknown') and employs an alcoholic agent to do the job. Miss Jordan is thus launched into a singing career, and although she is tone deaf, succeeds in making a record which is immediately rush-released. Trouble comes in the form of 'Legs' Wheeler, the juke box king; he refuses to play the record on his phonographs because he thinks that it's garbage. Wheeler, we discover, controls the juke boxes in four major East Coast cities, and nobody can be a star without his say-so.

Murdock isn't scared of anybody, and having received his early education in the slots during Prohibition, he knows how to handle the situation. He embarks on a tour of every location in New York, and this is his routine:

Fats and his henchman walk up to the barman, glowering. 'Where did you get your music box from?'

'Oh, that's a Wheeler Enterprises juke box, mister.'

(In unison) 'Oh yeh?'

Cut to Juke box crashing through window.

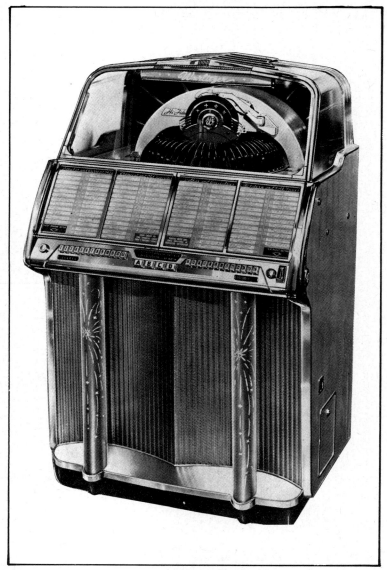

*Wurlitzer 1800 with 104 selections. (Courtesy M. Trussell)*

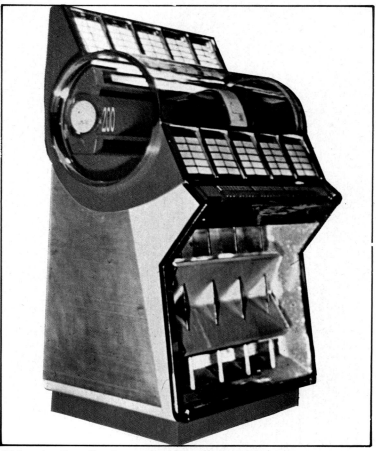

*200-selection Seeburg design, 1956. (Courtesy M. W. Kenney)*

In this manner, Murdock takes over much of Wheeler's territory and Jerry becomes a star. But will Wheeler take this lying down?

Cut to Wheeler's office.

*Wheeler:* 'How many juke boxes has Murdock removed?'

*Attorney*: 'Most of them round New York, and now he's making inroads into Boston, Philadelphia and Baltimore . . .

*Wheeler:* 'OK, that's far enough. You handle the legal side and I'll handle the inroads.'

Wheeler goes looking for Murdock with a gun in his pocket. Murdock is on his way to see Jerry (whom he is about to marry – with misgivings because he senses that she doesn't feel the same way about him) and Jerry is kissing the alcoholic agent in her dressing room (they've fallen in love with each other). Wheeler catches up with Murdock at the stage door, there is a fracas, and Murdock escapes to the one place where he is safe from the juke box fiend – on stage. He starts singing the number that he had composed for Jerry and Wheeler is so impressed that instead of shooting him, he signs him on. Jerry marries her agent and has three beautiful children. Fats get on the TV. Wheeler is still Mr Juke Box.

From the student's point of view, there are a few serious inconsistencies in this film. The P146s used were somewhat anachronistic, being at least five years too old for this setting. The producer was probably trying to cut costs and preferred to throw $30 machines out of the windows (especially if it took several takes). We would have been much happier with an M100B or even a Rock-Ola 'Fireball', and for the scene where the juke box is thrown down a flight of concrete steps, a Wurlitzer 1550 would have been nice.

The second inconsistency concerns the person of Mr 'Legs' Wheeler. The largest routes in America are about 450 locations usually within a ten-mile radius (a much smaller radius in a city), yet Mr Wheeler seemed to control tens of thousands (one imagines that some real operators sat through the movie several times trying to work out how Wheeler managed it). It is only by owning tens of thousands of jukeboxes that any one operator (or even a group) could substantially effect the sales of records. Wheeler is just a symbol of the combined power of the music industry and in no way resembles any persons or institutions within the music operating business. No single individual could ever use juke boxes to influence the sales of records. That is to say, he would not be eligible for 'payola' unless he had an impossibly large route.

This brings us back to the original question. 'Where's the Mob?' Of course, no one knows; but one has a sneaking suspicion that the myth of the Mob in juke boxes is fostered by those pillars of society who would prefer it not to be generally known that in reality, the Mob, if anywhere, is everywhere.

Outside America, the only country that has succeeded in manufacturing juke boxes on any scale is Germany. Even though Wurlitzer and Rock-Ola established factories over there, German juke boxes have won a sizeable portion of the European market, although few would argue that the indigenous product in any way compares with its American rival. England has a large but essentially American juke box population; the British have never mastered the art of production. A brief study of the UK industry will serve not only to underline the achievement of American business in this field, but will illustrate some of the basic attitudes that have been examined in this chapter.

*Far left: 'It's time you replaced your juke box.'*

*Left: Juke boxes are designed to withstand abuse, but this Seeburg P146 will not be playing any more music.*

*Below left: 'Legs' Wheeler – Mr Juke Box ('He was all heart').*

*Below: P146 rubbing shoulders with the public. (Stills from The Girl Can't Help It, courtesy Twentieth-Century Fox)*

# CHAPTER 18

## England

As with so many other aspects of the popular music industry, the influence of American thought and practice on the juke box in Britain has always been overwhelming. Mastery of the science of production was not one of the attributes Britain carried over from the nineteenth century into the twentieth, and a lack of competitiveness in the production of mass-market durables like juke boxes is particularly noticeable

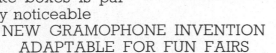

*Britain's 'Wondergram' of 1935.* (The World's Fair)

### NEW GRAMOPHONE INVENTION ADAPTABLE FOR FUN FAIRS

'Last week at the Grand Hotel, Sheffield, I attended a demonstration of a new invention which is described as "an almost human" gramophone . . . The demonstration was given to interested manufacturers, and it is probable that production on a mass scale will start shortly, probably in Sheffield, the home town of the inventor . . . When production starts, they are quite prepared to make record chambers to hold a hundred records if necessary . . . no price has yet been arranged.'

(*The World's Fair*, 20 July 1935)

'If necessary' – how exquisitely nonchalant! Fortunately for the American manufacturers, who managed to keep their cool about the whole thing, the 'Wondergram' went the way of all great British inventions, and no more was heard about it.

The manufacturers present at the demonstration may have decided that producing juke boxes was best left to the Yanks. Indeed, if any of them had conducted a market survey, they might well have decided that there was little sales potential for juke boxes in England in 1935; it had already been tried without success.

In 1932, the Samson Novelty Company of London were the largest importers of American arcade equipment and slot machines, being sole European agents for the Mills Novelty Company of Chicago. Mills had been manufacturing juke boxes for five years, and must have suggested to John Holloway of Samson the idea of placing an advertisement for a 'Dancemaster' in an English trade journal, to see if there was any reaction. Evidently, there was none, because the advertisement did not appear again. In 1935, Seeburg and Wurlitzer established agencies in England, and small advertisements started appearing in *The World's Fair* from about 1936. Judging by the scale of the promotion, the number of juke boxes imported at this time was very small. Coin men who were in business at the time have confirmed that there were less than a hundred juke boxes in England prior to 1937, and most of these were second-hand. In 1938-9, however, much more interest was being shown. The volume of business was growing, and for the first time, equipment was being shipped direct from the manufacturers.

It must be remembered that in the 1930s, the British coin machine industry was some little way behind its American cousin. Coin-operated equipment had still not graduated from the fairground to the High Street location, and operators were still, broadly speaking, regarded as showmen. Whatever potential the market was showing during the last years of peace, England was still not ready to receive the juke boxes into its cafes, clubs and public houses.

In any event, the war with Germany put a stop to the importation of non-essentials, and these restrictions were not lifted until 1955. For fifteen years, nine of them peacetime, the American manufacturers were effectively shut out of the UK

## talking about expansion-

It's a big subject. The rights and wrongs depend on the way you look at it.

**BUT WE ARE ONLY INTERESTED IN THE EXPANSION OF YOUR BUSINESS AND OUR BUSINESS.**

GROWTH MEANS PROGRESS — AND PROGRESS MEANS KEEPING ONE JUMP AHEAD OF THE OTHER FELLOW.

We have the young force, ideas and equipment to expand your business.

*Selling juke boxes in Africa? (Advertisement in* The World's Fair, *1936)*

*Wurlitzer 2000 – très chic. Several of these models came to Europe second hand during the mid-1950s.*

*These Wurlitzer 2300s might well have been awaiting shipment to England after the import restrictions had been lifted in 1957. Hundreds are still on location in Europe.*

market.

When the American Army moved its operational HQ to England, and the troops started arriving in their thousands, they brought with them a few basic luxuries that would serve to keep their morale up: *Esquire* magazines, pancake mix, baseball, Virginia tobacco and automatic phonographs.

Juke boxes were standard equipment in every PX. English operators, aware of this new market, brought juke boxes out of fairgrounds and off piers and relocated them in the clubs and public houses that the Yanks patronised. There were several Wurlitzer juke boxes in the Rainbow Room in Leicester Square, and it was a learning exercise for the English coin business.

The GIs were self-confident and outgoing, and made a powerful impact on the young English people with whom they came into contact – the way they dressed, talked, danced and even chewed gum. The Second World War was, in this respect, a global trades exhibition for American products.

When juke boxes first appeared in Germany and the Far East in the wake of the victorious US armies, they were a potent vehicle for Americanisation. As instruments of subliminal propaganda they were as effective as any amount of political indoctrination: there is nothing like a little music to help you to forget. Apart from the music, which had obvious appeal to the younger elements in those societies, the appearance of the juke box itself made an impression. They were, in 1941, at the very height of their art, and to the oriental eye, the model 850 would resemble a shrine or pulsating icon, rather than an everyday plaything. It is only when the object is removed from its context that it can be judged from a wholly aesthetic standpoint; in an art gallery today, or in Manila in 1946.

In 1946, Ditchburn, a Lancashire-based manufacturing company, negotiated a contract with Wurlitzer to manufacture the 'Simplex' mechanism in England. These sixteen-play record changers were encased in a plain wood-and-perspex cabinet that might have been mistaken for a refrigerator. It is highly unlikely that this phonograph would have been purchased by an American operator, even if it had been manufactured in 1933 when this mechanism was first used, but it met with great success in England. Ditchburn, like AMI, owned and operated their own equipment and confined their activities to the North of England. About two thousand of the 78rpm models were made, and they stayed in operation until they were replaced by American equipment at the end of the 1950s. One of the reasons they felt encouraged to operate for themselves was because there were no independent operators to whom they could sell the equipment. Ditchburn did, however, locate many of their machines in cafes and clubs, and this was an important development.

In 1952, Chantal Limited, a Bristol based firm, designed and constructed the first and only all-

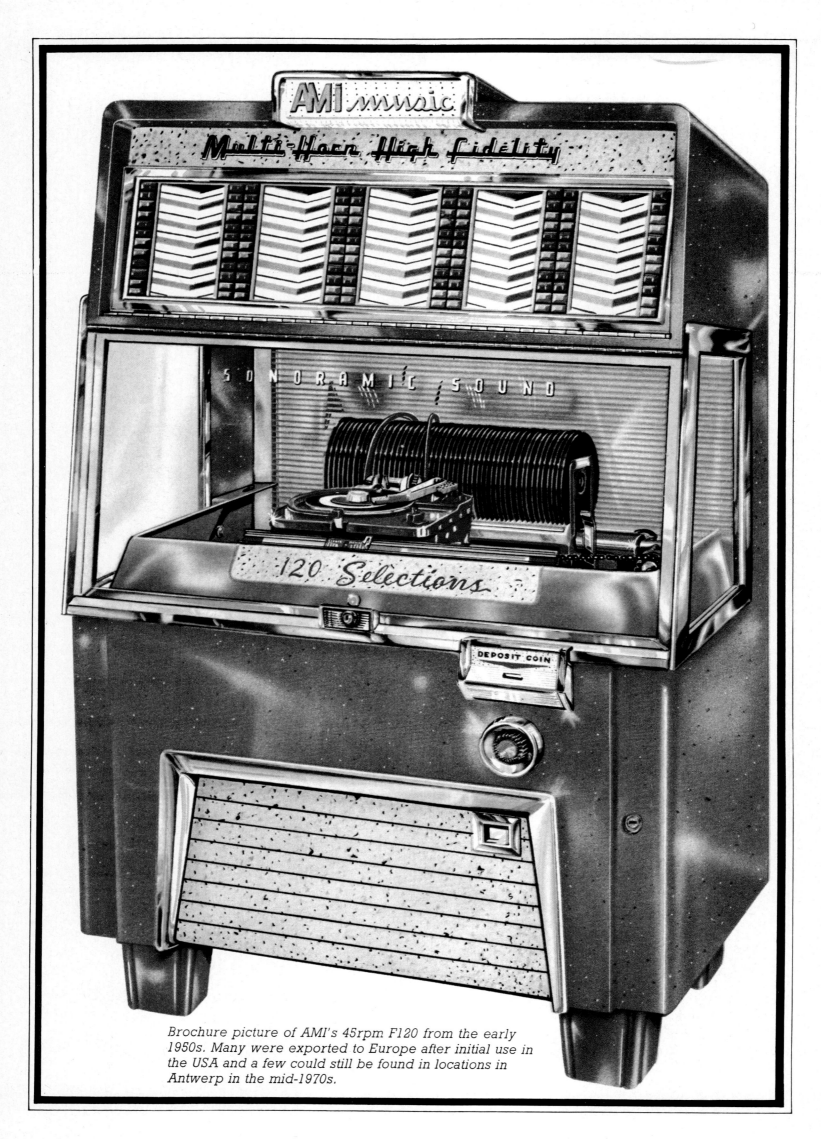

*Brochure picture of AMI's 45rpm F120 from the early 1950s. Many were exported to Europe after initial use in the USA and a few could still be found in locations in Antwerp in the mid-1970s.*

British juke box, the 'Meteor 200'. Their *modus operandi* was identical to that of Ditchburn, and they functioned in the South and South West of the country.

A hundred records, each clipped to a metal wheel, are stacked on a horizontal carousel with the tone arm and motor in the centre, the whole thing being encased in a transparent perspex hemisphere. The customer turns the carousel until the record he or she selects is in the middle of a kind of TV screen positioned at the front of the bubble. By pressing the numbered button, the solenoid is activated, pushing a key fractionally into the centre of the circle. As the motor and tone arm revolve in their own axis, they hit the key, the record is pushed forward and the wheel is engaged by the motor. It is possibly the simplest of all juke box selection mechanisms. Beneath the dome, the juke box tapers quite sharply to a triangular base with two small wooden legs of the type found on most furniture produced at the time. It was styled by David Fry. In retrospect, it is certainly the most distinctive juke box ever made.

When the import restrictions were lifted in 1956, and would-be operators had a choice between the Meteor 200 and an American machine, it was no contest. Many people in the trade found the Chantal weird-looking and, after the kids had smashed the dome a few times, expensive to maintain. The AMI G80, on the other hand, looked like a juke box. It had a row of buttons people could press – clearly it had been made by professionals. Mr Norman of Balfour Engineering, Ilford, Essex, had studied the import restrictions and noted that if 53% of the machine was British made, he could import the balance. After selecting AMI as the most suitable equipment for the UK market, he entered into an agreement with them whereby they shipped him some of the components, allowing him to manufacture the balance in England under licence, where the machine would be assembled. The model selected was the AMI G80, and it was renamed 'Bal Ami' on arrival. Although the machine was priced at £625 (this being more than double the list price in America), it was an instant success and marked the turning point for juke boxes in England. In two years Balfour sold as many juke boxes as had been manufactured and imported in the UK since 1935. *The World's Fair* opened its pages to this most popular arrival from America, and from 1957 devoted at least two pages of gossip, editorial and advertisements to the juke box. There was an air of genuine excitement in the industry, reminiscent of America in the month following the repeal of Prohibition.

But resistance to the juke box was much stronger in England than it ever had been in America, and town councillors even organised petitions against the invasion of their towns and villages. A latter-day juke box collector fondly recalls his first juke boxes:

'There was this cafe in Hitchin called the Copper Kettle. It was a milkshake parlour in the front,

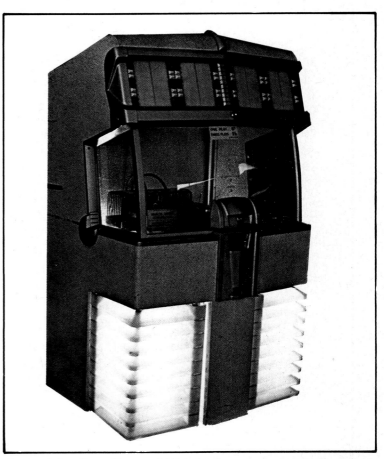

*One of the first 45rpm AMI juke boxes to reach England. (Courtesy Music Hire, Leeds/photo by Owen Smith)*

*The 'Music Maker', several thousand of which were manufactured in Lancashire by Ditchburn. This particular example once belonged to Billy Butlin, England's holiday camp magnate. (Burstein/Krivine)*

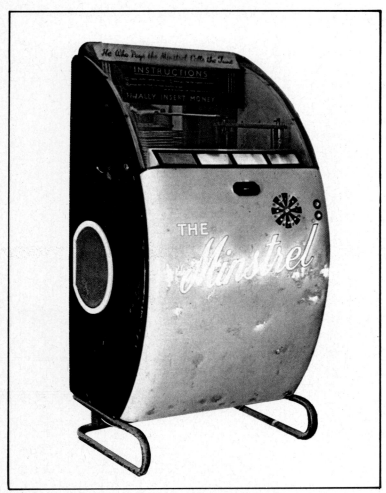

*The low-budget 'Minstrel' of 1952. (Courtesy Music Hire, Leeds/photo by Owen Smith)*

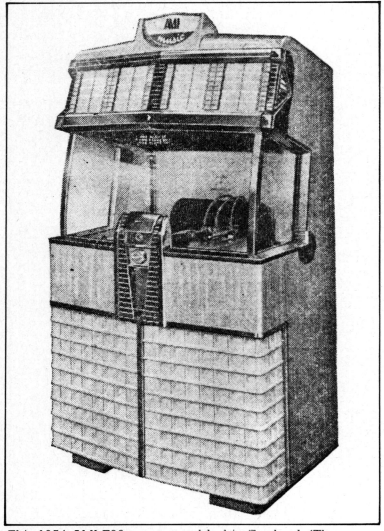

*This 1954 AMI E80 was assembled in England. (The World's Fair)*

and the back opened out into a wider area. it was a room without windows. There was an AMI "A" in the corner that had been converted to 45s. It played "Don't be Cruel" and "Heartbreak Hotel" and two other Presleys. I was a drop-out from grammar school, and I had a few of my mates with me. Apart from a dirty skylight, the juke box was the only light in the room. We took "Preludin" slimming pills – you could get them without a prescription but they killed your appetite. There was this mechanic stock car guy called Denny Coutt. He was the leader of the bike boys that went there. The Copper Kettle was the only cafe with a juke box in Hitchin. It was the only place we could smoke and listen to rock 'n' roll without being seen. I think the AMI came off the local US Air Force base. Another juke box I remember was a Seeburg. I was working up on the A1 between Stevenage and Baldock. I was assistant chef at Jack's Hill, on night shift. The lorry drivers wouldn't let you play it at night, they wanted peace and quiet. The operator was really pissed off about it.'

There was strong resistance from the business community. Operating a juke box in 1956 was tantamount to running an 'adult movie theatre' at the present time. Mr William Smith is today one of the leading figures in the juke box business; as well as distributing AMI equipment throughout England, he operates what is probably the largest juke box route in the world – fifteen hundred phonographs in the North and the Midlands. In 1956 he had a car showroom in the centre of Leeds:

'A man came to my car showroom wanting to buy an estate car – we were agents for Humber. He measured it up, but wasn't saying why. My sales manager, who was helping him at the time, got the impression that he was an undertaker, but didn't want to admit it. However, he duly bought it. He came in for a service. My sales manager was talking to him and he said: "Look, for a fair question, Mr Cheppelow, what are you going to do with the car? I can't understand it. Are you an undertaker?" So he said, "As a matter of fact, I sell juke boxes, but I didn't want to tell you." "With respect," said the salesman, "I'm shocked at you putting a juke box into a magnificent car like this," (it was a very expensive car at that time) and Mr Cheppelow said, "Well, I look at it from the profit angle, and let me tell you this, that the juke box is a lot more profitable than your motor trading".

'I happened to be passing at that moment, and my sales manager said to me: "Mr Smith, there is someone here in a more profitable business than we are. I think we should be in it." Jollying the customer along, that was all. However, Mr Cheppelow took it seriously and came in to see me and tried to persuade me to buy a juke box. Well, I was horrified. "Why not just try it. Your wife could go round on Saturday and collect the cash, tax free, all tax free. You know, they'll take £x per week will these juke boxes, fantastic".

' "No, never, I couldn't consider it." However he kept coming back and eventually said he

*A 1957 AMI. (Courtesy Music Hire, Leeds/photo by Owen Smith)*

A Wurlitzer 2400A as exported to England. (Acme Attractions)

Everybody's happy
(INCLUDING YOU!)
with the sensational, low cost
EMAPHONE
160 or 96 RECORDS

Low-budget, low-selling, English-manufactured juke box.

would put one on site for me, give me the keys and I could go and collect.

'I was quite impressed. My wife was very much against it until she realised how profitable it was.

'We eventually came to an arrangement whereby he found the site and serviced the machine, while I did the collections and changed the records every fortnight. If the site was satisfactory after two collections, I bought the machine. These were marvellous days. He could go out and find sites just like that. This went on for about thirty machines. I realised I was in a fairly profitable business. The site owner was happy with a very nominal commission. On the other hand, there was opposition to juke boxes.

'Mr Cheppelow was AMI distributor for northern England. His problem was in finding people to buy and operate the equipment. Any respectable firm would not touch them, and less respectable firms could not get HP [credit].

'My wife did not want me to tell our friends that we were bothering with juke boxes, because it was so degrading. She would not even tell our cleaner.

'In those early days, we financed ourselves. We were lucky. We were giving HP companies a lot of business through the motor trade – we were on good terms with Lloyds and Scottish. Their local manager trusted me. He said, ''Well Bill, I trust your judgement,'' and because of that we were able to expand.

1958 novelty juke box with monkeys playing instruments. Not surprisingly, very few were made. (The World's Fair)

*One of the factors that retarded the development of the industry in the U K* (The World's Fair)

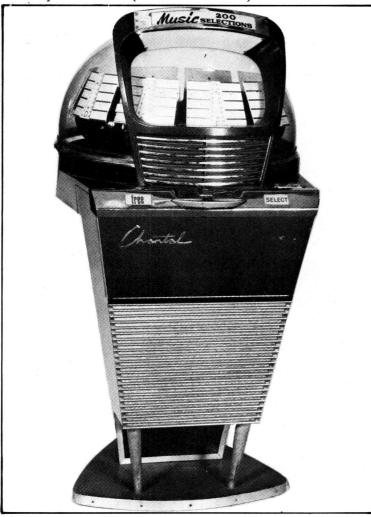

*The Chantal 'Meteor', styled by David Fry and built in Bristol between 1952 and 1959. (Courtesy Sotheby & Co, London)*

# THE NATION'S
# TOP TEN
## JUKE-BOX TUNES

A list of the ten most-played discs in juke boxes, compiled from information supplied by juke-box owners and operators throughout the country.

| Last week | This week | | |
|---|---|---|---|
| 1 | 1 | BUTTERFLY | Andy Williams |
| 4 | 2 | ROCK-A-BILLY | Guy Mitchell |
| 2 | 3 | CUMBERLAND GAP | The Vipers |
| 8 | 4 | WHEN I FALL IN LOVE | Nat "King" Cole |
| 7 | 5 | FREIGHT TRAIN | Chas. McDevitt Skiffle Gp. |
| — | 6 | YES, TONIGHT JOSEPHINE | Johnnie Ray |
| 6 | 7 | TOO MUCH | Elvis Presley |
| — | 8 | I'LL TAKE YOU HOME AGAIN KATHLEEN | Slim Whitman |
| 5 | 9 | BABY, BABY | The Teenagers |
| 3 | 10 | NINETY-NINE WAYS | Tab Hunter |

*A 1957 juke box top ten as recorded in* The World's Fair. *Such charts often differed appreciably from those based on record sales.*

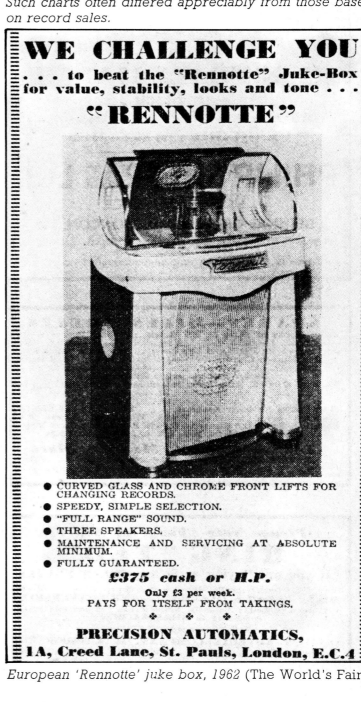

*European 'Rennotte' juke box, 1962* (The World's Fair)

*A 1961 AMI 'Continental', still on location in the north of England in 1975. (Owen Smith)*

'In 1956–7, no brewery would consider having a juke box in a pub. Today, there is nothing worth considering except the breweries. Cafes and clubs are not worth a light nowadays. Eventually, we persuaded Whitbreads of Sheffield – that was the breakthrough. The first one we got was a very busy working-class pub called the Barley Corn. Mr Tushingham and I walked in with the juke box and the manager was there waiting for us. But there was Sam and Lill, two awful entertainers. Well, we walked in with the juke box and their faces fell a mile when they saw it. We installed it and walked out. We learned later that they didn't perform there any more because everyone wanted to listen to the juke box. It was a novelty in a pub. A week later, we spoke to Whitbread's; they said. ''Yes, it's going well, we'll try another, have a look at Lady's Bridge''. We arrived one evening – it was all evening work – and there were Sam and Lill doing their turn, you see. We wheeled the juke box in and they were out of a job again. Then we went to a third Whitbread pub to install a third juke box and there was Sam and Lill again. We did this at four pubs chasing Sam and Lill out. I don't know what happened to them – I've always felt sorry for this rather aged couple . . . '

By the 1960s, the juke box was fully integrated into the fabric of English life. Although it is quite possible that the British would have developed a coin-operated phonograph without the initiative from America, the extent to which it has been accepted by this society is a measure of England's 'Americanisation'. Indeed, in the late 1950s it became popular because of its identification with American styles. In this respect, the juke box is a cultural barometer.

*Singer Joe Brown accompanied by a German phonograph in the film* What a Crazy World. *(Courtesy Associated British Film)*

*AMI late 1960s 'New Yorker'. (Courtesy Music Hire, Leeds/photo by Owen Smith)*

Explicit advertising for the 'Fanfare', an early 1960s German juke box successfully marketed in Britain. (The World's Fair)

# JUKE BOX ON TRIAL

IN spite of opposition from the police, Chipping Norton, Oxon., magistrates, have granted an extension of the music licence at the town's Regent Cinema snack bar from 8 p.m. until 10 p.m. The new licence has been granted on a year's trial.

The cafe manageress, Mrs. M. J. Messenbird, had made the application for the extension, supported by a petition containing 120 names. The music is supplied by a record player.

For Mrs. Messenbird, Mr. R. G. Boulton said the music was played at variable tone and volume and it was the intention of the proprietor to instal a volume control behind the snack bar so that the sound could be regulated to a reasonable level. The snack bar was not situated in a closely built-up residential area.

### "Fatal" Fascination

Mr. Boulton said that this type of music seemed to have a rather fatal fascination for the young 18 to 19-year-old but he did not see anything objectionable in that. He did not see that this sort of music was conducive to any kind of immoral behaviour.

For the police, Superintendent N. G. Brown said that the sound of the peculiar and eccentric music thumped out on juke boxes might be a trial to elderly or mature people living in the vicinity.

"To be quite frank," said Superintendent Brown, "nice young people do not go to these places after 8 p.m. It is my experience that where these licences are granted after eight o'clock nothing but trouble can arise for the people who manage these places and for the police who try to maintain order."

### Cafe Renovated

The cafe was rented by Mr. John G. Messenbird, who said it was recently renovated throughout and good meals were served. He said that the music was an attraction for young people who went to the public houses after the snack bar juke box had closed down. He felt they were better off in the snack bar.

He added that the snack bar was looked upon as a youth club. The young people sat over a cup of coffee all evening and there was no noise when the juke box was played. There had been no complaints from neighbours.

As stated, the licence was granted on a year's trial.

Even as late as October 1957, when The World's Fair published this article, conservative elements in England retarded general acceptance of the juke box.

# Hymn Played on Juke Box

AT the funeral on Monday of Graham Wilson (19), of Salts Street, Shaw, Lancs., killed last week in a motor cycle accident, the cortege stopped outside the cafe where he and his friends were in the habit of congregating and, accompanied by a record played on the cafe juke-box, his friends, mill operatives, housewives, and others watching the funeral, joined in singing the hymn "Abide With Me." The cafe—on Market Street, Shaw—is a regular rendezvous for young motorcyclists in the district.

News item in The World's Fair, October 1957.

German makers found a lucrative market in Britain. This ad for the 'Tonmaster' appeared in September 1959. (The World's Fair)

# CHAPTER 19

## 1960 Onwards

B Y THE mid-1950s, the juke box had gone as far as it could go. There was one machine for every 330 Americans. Seeburg, Rock-Ola and Wurlitzer were household names and the 8000 operators throughout the country were ordering records at the rate of 74,000,000 per year.

In the following two decades, the industry did not keep pace with the general process of growth and expansion. The ratio of juke boxes to the population fell to 1 : 530 and, whereas the increase in output of other durables such as refrigerators, TVs, automobiles and pinball machines almost doubled, the production of juke boxes actually dropped by between ten and twenty per cent, although this was more than compensated for by the opening up of overseas markets.

*A. D. Palmer, Wurlitzer's advertising and sales promotion manager from 1949 to 1974 and now the official historian of the company.*

The health of the industry can be measured by the profitability of the operator. For him, things are not as they once were.

'To get a location today, you've got to offer the location owner a contract; he might get three or four operators in and they are all making solicitations for the location. He will be looking for a good commission, bonuses, maybe a loan and other things. In the 1930s, the location owners wanted juke boxes and it didn't cost you a thing . . . you give him a piece of equipment and then you set up a commission arrangement, nothing else, there was no advance money like today. It has developed into a very tough business; you have got to have capital today.'

Meyer Parkoff is suggesting that the operators' share of the total revenue has been reduced to the advantage of the location owner, but even more significant is that the revenue itself has fallen over the years. Some argue that the price of a play (25c in many locations today) is too high. The industry has promoted this tendency in order to help the operator who now has to pay almost

$2000 for new equipment. In real terms, however, the value of a quarter today is the equivalent of a nickel in the 1930s and the equipment itself is subject to exactly the same inflationary processes as the rest of the economy. Another possible factor is the longer playing time of popular records today; fifteen years ago, it was possible to get twenty plays per hour, but in 1975, the average had fallen to sixteen. This alone would account for a 20% loss of income. Operators have had to diversify in order to stay in business and today it is rare to find a juke box operator who doesn't have amusement machines and vending equipment on his route. In this context the word 'juke box' has assumed a wider meaning to include the whole coin-operated music and amusement industry.

There are, however, more fundamental reasons for the relative decline of the juke box.

The degeneration of America's city centres, euphemistically known as 'urban renewal', has resulted in the loss of prime juke box locations, as the population has moved out into the suburbs. In the taverns and eating houses that remain, the juke box is an obvious target for junkies and delinquents, and reinforced cash doors, steel bars and extra locks are standard equipment in certain locations. In Liverpool, England, vandalism has forced juke boxes out of many of the public houses in the city centre.

The 'fast-food' concept has also undermined the position of the juke box. The diner, the roadside cafe and the corner drug store were traditional locations for a phonograph. The travelling public could park their cars and sit down in an eating house for a meal which would be served at a table and would last for about one hour. The customer was encouraged to take his time, play the juke box and engage in conversation. This social convention has largely been replaced by a

*Rock-Ola model 403 wall phonograph, 1964. (Courtesy Rock-Ola Manufacturing Corporation)*

new concept in eating in which the massive catering organisations like McDonalds, Jack-in-the-Box and Burger King have played a major role. The atmosphere is clean, pleasant but not warm. The patron is encouraged to purchase his food as if it were groceries, eat it quickly and get back into his car.

The other type of catering conglomerate such as Ramada Inn, Howard Johnson, Trust House Forte (UK) and Mecca (UK), where the patron is able to relax and eat at a more leisurely rate, has positively refused to countenance a juke box, preferring pre-recorded tapes with soporific instrumental muzak programmes. Although the powerful catering cartels control the services on the major highways in America and Europe, the old-fashioned eating house can still be found on the secondary road systems and most of them have retained coin-operated music.

The club location has to a large extent replaced the juke box with the discotheque. The location owner is prepared to sacrifice the income from a juke box and purchase expensive sound equipment of his own, with the additional cost of a disc jockey, because the public now demands a sound quality, degree of volume and style of presentation that the juke box cannot provide. It is extremely rare nowadays to see a couple dancing in front of a juke box. When Seeburg introduced its first quadrophonic system in 1975, it was hailed as 'a major breakthrough in audio concept'. It could better be described as a rearguard action; Seeburg were simply responding of necessity to initiatives from elsewhere in the audio industry.

The same holds true of another advance in the field of sound technology, stereo, which came in the 1950s. The concept of sound separation was not designed with the juke box in mind. As the public developed a taste for increased realism and invested in sophisticated components for their home record players, standards of reproductive quality were set with which the juke box could not compete. The juke box industry jumped on to the bandwagon, but since all the speakers were mounted in one cabinet, the stereophonic value remained as low as that of the domestic integrated radiogram. If the speakers of a juke box are amputated and dispersed in two or even four distant corners of a room, to what extent is the 'control box' still a juke box? Seeburg suggests it is a 'total entertainment centre' which is sufficiently nebulous to fit the bill.

The greatest single threat to the juke box in the post-war period has been television. This is the thing that keeps millions of Americans home in the evenings; it is the dominant entertainment medium of the age and at various times has threatened to take over completely. The TV is everywhere, even in juke box locations. When a ball game is televised, the phonograph is turned off.

Conscious of this unequal contest, many companies attempted to manufacture the television-juke box or video juke box. As early as 1947, Mills brought out the 'Panorama' which proved too expensive to be practical. There have been over a dozen video boxes produced since then, and the only one that achieved any measure of success was the 'Scopitone' and that was short-lived. The French produced a model in 1960 that was marketed in Europe and was fairly popular in England at the time. The fundamental shortcoming of the video juke box concept is the fact that the public doesn't want to have to watch the juke box as an audience; the function of the juke box is to provide background music for talking, drinking or dancing and the video box fails to take this into account. In any event the novelty quickly wears off.

In the 1950s, the juke box had been both vehicle and focus for a youth culture. It was a 'place' away from the home environment, where kids could meet and listen to the music of their idols. It was the subject of songs, poems and films of the time, and had a meaning that went far beyond its function of mere music machine; it was a symbol of teenage independence.

In the 1960s, a reaction set in, not just to the 1950s, but to a succession of cultural impulses that culminated in that colourful decade. It was a rebellion of a forceful and coherent nature which, in its more extreme manifestations, amounted to a rejection not only of certain styles and mores, but of the American way of life itself. It began on the West Coast as a minor sub-culture which was experimenting with an alternative life-style based on anti-materialism, good will and soft drugs. As a style, it caught on, spreading east and across the Atlantic, mutating perceptibly as it grew. From a humble philosophical hypothesis, it developed into a major movement that had its roots in the college campuses of America. The youth polarised themselves into a position of opposition, and in the process of turning the traditional values upside down, they evolved an original style and expression that was subsequently adopted by society at large. In this so-called 'revolution', the juke box had no place. It had become too closely identified with the 1950s to survive the process of rejection, and as the exciting musical developments of the 1960s unfolded, the coin-operated phonograph stood in the wings.

The new music, compared to the playful banality of early rock lyrics, was intense and 'meaningful'. Composers like Lennon-McCartney ('the greatest songwriters since Schubert') and Dylan produced albums of such a consistently high standard that the public developed a preference for long-playing records of rock music. The LP had, up till then, been much more attuned to classical music; in 1967, for the first time, rock albums began to sell more than 45s. The recording industry took this into account and were promoting music that was just not suitable for juke boxes – fifteen-minute songs became commonplace. They capitalised on the proliferation of stereophonic record player components, and the artwork on record covers was, in many cases, outstanding. After sixty years, the emphasis was on home phonographs once more.

*Seeburg 'Discothèque', 1965. (Courtesy K. Baxter)*

The position of the dope-smoking youth in 1967 was similar to that of the boozers during prohibition. If you wanted to hear progressive rock music with a joint in your hand, that was two good reasons why you wouldn't do it in a tavern.

The effect of soft drugs on kids at that time was to make them more introspective, less extrovert, nominally more aware. Many had the opportunity to travel to Europe and the Far East and foreign influences began to appear on the American scene; for example, English rock music, German products (the Volkswagen automobile was extraordinarily popular at this time) and some of the less austere features of Oriental philosophy. The Vietnam war gave American youth a very personal interest in politics and the anti-war movement became a dominant theme in contemporary music. All this was happening without the help of the juke box; one need only listen to a few fifties songs like 'Truck Drivin' Man', 'School Days' and 'Roll Over Beethoven' to realise how central the juke box had been. In sixties lyrics it vanished without trace.

Despite its absence from youth culture, the fact that the juke box industry came through the 1960s undiminished in numbers of companies involved is surely proof of the existence of the mythical silent majority. There were still plenty of Americans left who drank beer and dropped dimes and quarters into the juke box like their fathers did before them. Nevertheless, that rejection by the younger generation, the group which had always been the juke box's most ardent supporter, unquestionably had a demoralising effect on the industry. When the crunch came in 1973 with America's worst economic recession since World War Two, Seeburg experienced severe financial stress from which it has still not fully recovered, and Wurlitzer went out of business.

The story of Wurlitzer's collapse is worth recording. In the late 1960s they produced machines that were below their usual standard and which did not meet with the approval of the operators. They were a very large diversified organisation and were able to take a long cool look at the situation. Juke boxes, they felt, were on the way out. There were more sophisticated forms of automatic entertainment available which would in time displace the phonograph altogether. In the short term, the phonograph division would be kept open so long as it paid its own way, but the Wurlitzer executives were not prepared to invest large sums on new plant and machinery in order to remain in a business which they considered had a limited future. In 1972, the end was near. The phonograph division made one last effort; the model 1050.

In the early 1970s, there was a fashion for 'nostalgia'. Designers were getting their ideas from old Hollywood movies, and Art Deco, having been utterly rejected during the 1950s and 1960s, was being rediscovered. The Wurlitzer design team was acutely aware of the doldrums into which their art had fallen, and decided to indulge in a little nostalgia of their own. The model 1050 was conceived not as a copy of the 1015, but as 'a modern interpretation' of the style. A replica, apart from being impossibly expensive, would have looked odd in a modern tavern.

When the 1050 was unveiled at the distributor's meeting in 1973, many of the old-timers and their wives were so moved by the sight of this machine that they broke down in tears; it was such a powerful reminder of the good old days. In point of fact, the 1050 was a dismal failure as far as the operators were concerned, and before the end of the year, Wurlitzer announced its retirement from the American juke box industry. Its passing was mourned by many.

At the time of writing, the juke box is still a major factor in the coin-machine industry, and some say that there will always be a juke box. This may well be true, but the listeners will no longer be the high-school kids who couldn't wait (in Chuck Berry's song) to get out of school and down to the juke-joint, there to dance and make romance. They will be the poor and middle-class whites, in city-centre bars and in road houses and truck stops out along the great highways of America, listening to the old songs and the newer country licks of Charley Pride and Waylon Jennings. Probably they won't even notice when the juke box is taken out and the muzak piped in. This study tails off in the late 1950s because it was at about that time that the juke box lost what David Slovic has called 'specialness of place'. Until that point, there had been over thirteen hundred American Saturday nights that would not have been the same without the juke box. They were the product of an environment that now no longer exists.

*Wurlitzer's last juke box, the heavily nostalgic 1050. (Owen Smith)*

*A Seeburg 'Console'. (Courtesy K. Baxter)*

# APPENDIX:
## Notes on Design and Styling

In Victor Paparnek's book, *Design for the Real World*, H. Van Doren describes the role of the industrial designer in the following way:

'It is the practice of analysing, creating and developing products for mass manufacture. Its goal is to achieve forms which are assured of acceptance before extensive capital investment has been made and which can be manufactured at a price permitting wide distribution and reasonable profits.'

The search for the 'right' form can be a very exacting occupation, requiring innumerable sketches, drawings and models that must be approved by different people within the organisation, but essentially, it is more a calculation than a creation. In the case of an aircraft, performance is paramount; the appearance, which in any event is dictated by engineering considerations, is relatively unimportant. The Boeing 747 might, at first sight, appear a trifle ungainly, but once the public realises that it is safe, comfortable and fast, they soon grow to like it. Volkswagen's Beetle is an ugly car, but its performance is such that its basic design has remained unchanged for forty years. An electric kettle has only to look like an electric kettle; if it is efficient, it has every chance of selling well.

The performance of a juke box, however, is less exacting. Once a selection mechanism was built, it served the manufacturer for an average of twenty years. Wurlitzer produced almost sixty models using the basic 'Simplex' design, and AMI used their system for almost thirty years, from 1927 until the early 1950s. It would be true to say that, compared to an aircraft or an automobile, the mechanical requirements are minimal (the Seeburg M100 was an exception to this rule). Since there is little to choose between the performance of one juke box and another, the public (and the operator) must choose the product on the basis of its appearance; therefore, the role of the designer in this industry has been primary.

The juke box is different from many products in that it must project a definite image to the public. Because it is a medium for entertainment, it must look the part. Since it is provided for the enjoyment of leisure, it must look cheerful. Even if its surroundings are not always colourful,

expensive and sophisticated, it must look glamorous. In the industry, this ingredient is known as 'flash'.

Van Doren's definition therefore is inadequate when it comes to the juke box. It must not only be 'accepted', it must be loved, enjoyed and appreciated. It must be so compelling that the public will want to approach it, touch it and put money into it.

The attraction, however, is of an ephemeral nature. The public develops a jaded familiarity with the machine and grows bored with its appearance. At this point, the shrewd operator will replace the juke box with a newer model which will trigger off new feelings of excitement, once again compelling the public to draw near. And so it goes on. This works to the advantage of the manufacturer who is constantly called upon to produce more equipment.

The designer or 'stylist' is involved in a highly creative activity. His job resembles that of a fashion designer, who must keep producing new ideas each season, but must remain within the confines of his clients' own perceptions; they must not be too outrageous. By the same token, the juke box must always look like a juke box. George Kubler, in his book *The Shape of Time* is discussing 'aesthetic fatigue':

'The artist himself is most exposed to tedium, overcoming it by the invention of new formal combinations and by more daring advances in previously established directions. These advances obey a rule of gradual differentiation because they must remain as recognisable variations upon the dominant memory image.'

The Rock-Ola 'Spectravox' was an example of a juke box that was not a 'recognisable variation', and partly for that reason, it was a commercial failure.

Whatever value latter-day collectors place upon their juke box, to the men who made them, they were just 'pieces of equipment'. Concerning the 1015 model, Fred Osborne, Wurlitzer engineer during the 1940s, said to me that my 'opinion that it was an outstanding artistic success is one of the things that makes horse races. It was a nice box, sure.'

Homer E. Capehart said, 'I don't know about

*5308 Wurlitzer 2700s were manufactured in 1962-3. (Courtesy M. Trussell)*

art. We sold plenty.'

In his book *Diners*, David Slovic draws a distinction between conscious and unconscious design.

'The most revealing products of any culture are the ones that are not consciously designed. Design demands a self-consciousness which removes the designer from the object and from its cultural aspirations . . . [The diner] is unconsciously designed by artists who work in factories.'

The artists in this case are not just the designers, but the entire company which includes the workers, the salesmen, the directors and the engineers who pool their respective skills into an enterprise, the end product of which is a diner or a juke box. This is, to use Bernard Rudowski's expression, 'non-pedigreed' art. If it sold well, it was good. If it sold badly, it was a dog.

The juke box, remember, is a coin-operated machine and every operator knows that when the patron drops a coin, he wants to see something happen; this makes it a novelty. The juke box provides this service by making the selection mechanism clearly visible through a glass window at the front of the machine. Wurlitzer and Rock-Ola exploited this appealing feature by chrome-plating all the moving parts of the record changer and providing a decorative backdrop to dramatise the scene. Wurlitzer designed rainbows, peacock feathers and elaborate montages

*Wurlitzer 'Statesman', mid-1960s. (Courtesy M. Trussell)*

146

with theatrical 'curtains' pulled back to underline the image. Rock-Ola preferred pastoral or classical themes, like a balcony with a Venetian sunset. The public was getting value for money.

The nickel is deposited; instantly the lights flash on and the selection panel is brightly illuminated. Press a button and the solenoid is activated . . . Bzzzz! Click! . . . Deep in the bowels of the cabinet, a motor whirrs to life, and a metal finger can be seen rising slowly on the central spindle, searching for the record that has been selected. Click! It stops; the metal tray swings out in a wide arc, exposing a shiny black shellac disc. It stops when it has reached across the changer, inches below the expectant tone arm. Down below, the camshaft has completed its revolution and suddenly the main motor engages the turntable which quickly gathers momentum as it rises steadily, picks up the record from its tray and bears it upward to the wide chromium 15oz tone arm. The stylus makes contact with the disc and soon all mechanical sounds are drowned out by a pregnant hiss as the needle seeks out the first bar of the melody. The whole thing takes ten seconds.

The earliest juke boxes, such as the 'Orchestrope', derived their appearance from contemporary home phonographs of the more expensive variety, plain, solid and wooden. When Capehart had joined up with Wurlitzer, he made use of the available skills at North Tonawanda and attempted to make the phonograph into a fine

*Wurlitzer 'Americana', early 1970s.*

piece of furniture.

'[Capehart] requested alcohol lacquer on flat surfaces where a patron might spill a drink. With a glossy shine, Capehart remembered telling the boys, the Simplex would less resemble a "coffin standing on its end".'

(Pickett)

In the early 1930s, the radio had replaced the phonograph as the dominant musical medium in America, and the juke boxes resembled outsize radios complete with bakelite knobs and switches on the front. By 1937–8, the manufacturers realised that in order to maintain output, a still greater effort was required. One of the directions that this competitive intensification took was in the styling of the equipment.

Ray Haimbaugh, chief engineer at North Tonawanda, was one of an informal committee of 'designers', which included everybody from Farny Wurlitzer to the cabinet makers, and he was not happy with the slap-happy approach that was being taken to the problem of styling. He knew a young man called Paul Fuller who was beginning to make his name as a designer, and after conferring with Capehart, offered Fuller a job at the factory. The designer hesitated; he was not sure if he wanted to design furniture, and in 1934, juke boxes were a singularly dull prospect. Jobs, however, were scarce at that time and he finally agreed to work on the three models for 1935 on a contract basis. These were the P12, P400 and P30. It proved a successful arrangement

*1970s Rock-Ola model 456, designed by James Sullivan.*

for all concerned and in that year he became a full-time employee of the company.

Paul Fuller, born in Switzerland in 1899, emigrated to the United States in his early twenties. Having studied furniture design after leaving school, he wanted to travel for a few years and on arriving in New York, he journeyed west. Very little is known about his life at this time, but the story goes that he was working on a ranch in Montana where the ranch owner's wife took a fancy to the young traveller and tried to teach him English. His textbook was an outdated Sears-Roebuck catalogue which at the same time gave him a useful introduction to American design. At some point, he went back East and took a job in Chicago with Marshal Field, which was then the most elegant department store in America. He was both talented and hard-working and became the head of the interior design department before he was thirty.

In 1933, he found an opportunity to go freelance; the World Fair was being held in Chicago that year, and one of the exhibits was to be a restaurant on ice. The organisers wanted an 'Alpine' atmosphere, and Fuller had the natural qualification. The finished product was called 'The Black Forest Exhibit' and it was a great success.

When Fuller joined Wurlitzer, if the work wasn't over-stimulating, at least the atmosphere was congenial and the pay was good. He worked well with wood and succeeded in giving the cabinets

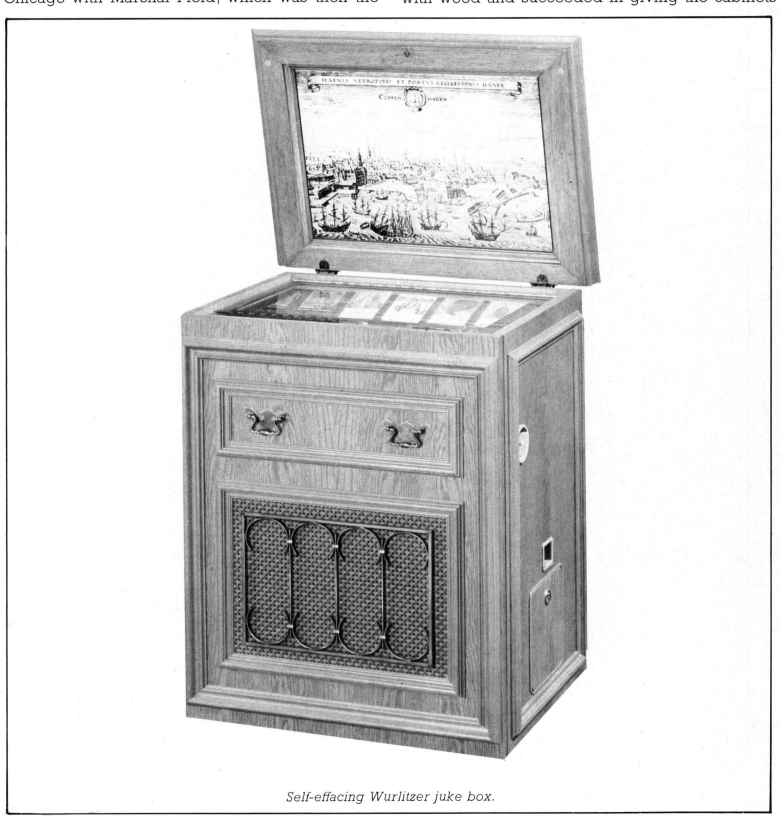

*Self-effacing Wurlitzer juke box.*

that little extra that distinguished them from their competitors. In 1938, Nils Miller of Seeburg had introduced translucent plastics into his cabinets and, according to one source, Wurlitzer and Rock-Ola scrapped their designs for that year in order to incorporate this new concept. Although there is firm evidence that Capehart was experimenting with lucite in 1937, this does not necessarily conflict with the story, and the credit for this important innovation must go to Miller. However, once Fuller got hold of this new medium, there was no stopping him.

He was given a special enclosure in the factory into which only a handful of people were allowed. Mr Carlson explained that 'there was something in coming out with ideas before anyone else'.

and by all accounts, there was a fair amount of industrial espionage in this business. When Wurlitzer introduced a new line – every one to two years – it was in batches of about eight models, incorporating three of four totally new concepts in styling. This was calculated to cover every operating possibility, and the prices were set accordingly. Fuller was both liked and respected within the organisation and was allowed to get on with his work without interference. As Carlson put it:

'When Paul had done his work, he just came out and said, "here it is", and we went ahead and made it. He never spoke to the distributors to find out what they wanted, or listened to what the district managers had to say . . . that's where we

*Seeburg 'Bandshell 160' for the 1970s market.*

went wrong later.'

In 1939, Wurlitzer continued with the highly successful models 500, 600 and counter model 61; they were conserving their resources for a special drive that was planned for the spring of 1940. In that year Paul Fuller did his finest work, producing eleven new models of which seven were distinct concepts. These were two new counter models, the 700, 800, 750, 780, and 850 (the 'Peacock'). Between them, Wurlitzer shipped about 60,000 phonographs in the period leading up to Pearl Harbour.

It is possible to speculate that the model 1015 was planned for 1942; it leads on so naturally from the 780 and 750E that it is hard to believe that six years separate them. The fact that the 1015 was devoid of any military flavour (compared to the Seeburg 'turret' of 1946, the Wurlitzer 'bomber-nose' (1100) and the Rock-Ola 'Rocket' of 1950) would suggest that it was conceived before the jingoism began. As it was, Fuller was not hard pressed during the war, and was responsible for only one juke box creation, the 'Victory' universal cabinet. It had a heavily romantic flavour.

Paul Fuller's last juke box was the model 1100. Through no fault of his own, Wurlitzer had come unstuck in 1948 and the atmosphere at North Tonawanda must have been somewhat tense. Joseph Clement who succeeded Fuller as director of design described Paul's last years in a letter written to the author in 1975.

'I was hired by Paul Fuller and Ray Haimbaugh

*Seeburg 'Entertainer', 1975-6.*

to be their chief designer – starting in January of '46. Paul was director of design and I had four designers and a model shop group responsible to Paul. The juke box model 1015 was being produced currently and Paul had started another concept called the 1100 model. This is where I entered juke box designing in earnest.

'I soon realised that Paul had had a heart attack prior to my appearance on the scene and was constantly under doctors' care . . . much of the work fell on my shoulders. Paul neglected his health by defying the doctors' orders and his wife's [Ruby, Fuller's second wife]; he loved to eat and our trips out together consisted of visiting the best restaurants – which Paul would select.

'From 1947–8 Wurlitzer went through some turbulent times . . . my department was discontinued and my services terminated. Paul remained at Wurlitzer, looking very despondent when I said goodbye.

'In 1950, Paul left Wurlitzer and bought a small wood-case manufacturing company making silverware chests in Onieda, N.Y. His heart problem restricted his design activities and the small company was in trouble. One day I received a call from Paul asking me to come and work for him. Ruby said he was calling from his sick bed and needed help. I told Paul I would write him a letter – not wanting to hurt him by declining immediately over the phone. He never saw the letter when it arrived – he died the next day. Paul was 53 years old when he died.

*Post-psychedelic Rock-Ola 464, 1975-6.*

*A last look back at some of Paul Fuller's classic 1940 creations. This is the Wurlitzer 800 of 1940. 11,501 were manufactured. (Courtesy Bob Plotnick)*

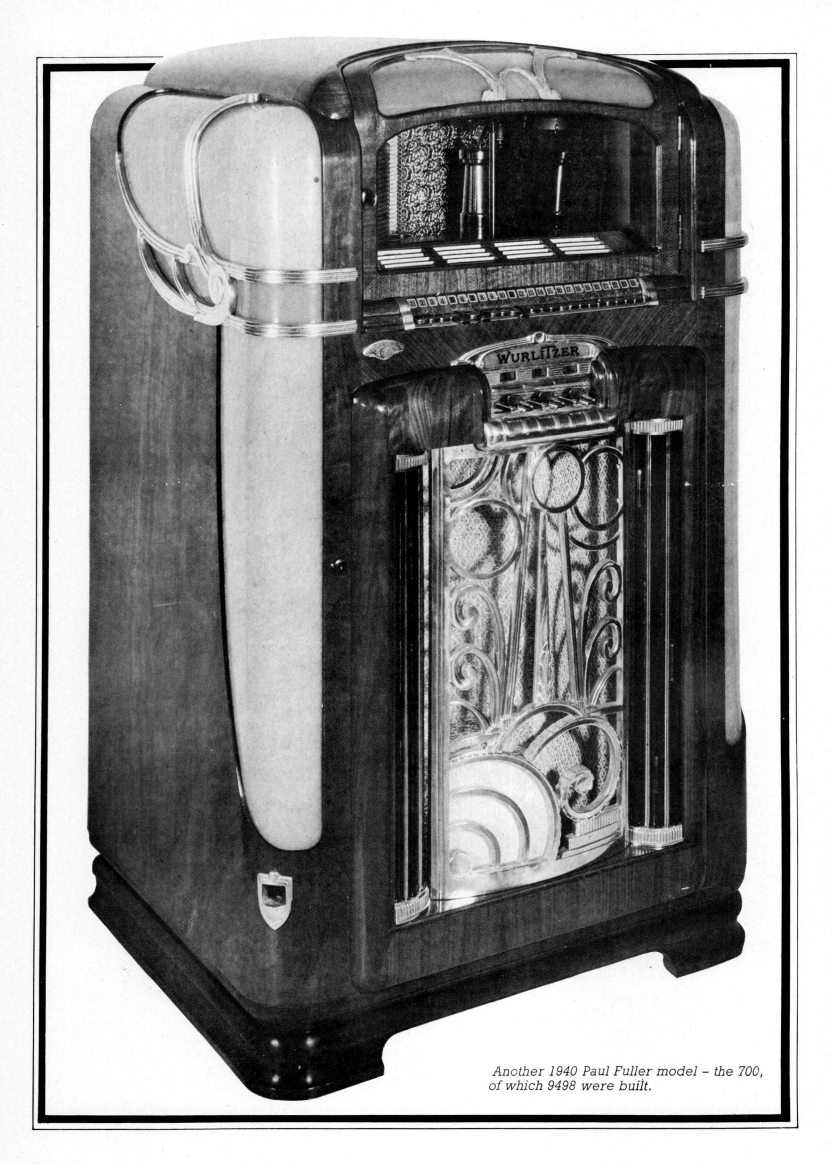

Another 1940 Paul Fuller model – the 700,
of which 9498 were built.

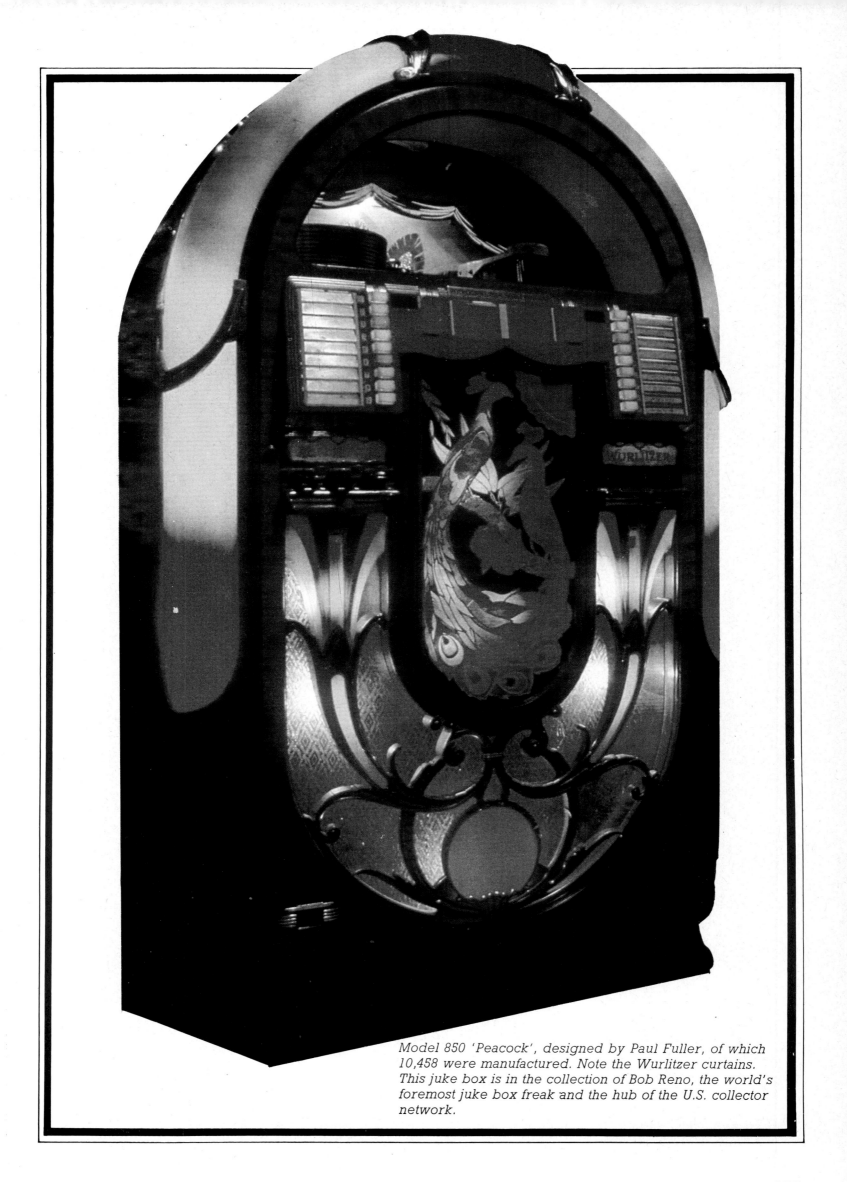

*Model 850 'Peacock', designed by Paul Fuller, of which 10,458 were manufactured. Note the Wurlitzer curtains. This juke box is in the collection of Bob Reno, the world's foremost juke box freak and the hub of the U.S. collector network.*

'The Wurlitzer company's juke box division was in deep trouble; Paul was gone, and the cabinets as styled by the engineering department were not selling. Their annual sales were the worst in their history.

'It was at that time that Ray Haimbaugh who was vice-president in charge of the North Tonawanda plant in New York State asked me if I would be interested in designing juke boxes again.

'I had to come up with a new cabinet design, using the old changer mechanism – and with a very short production deadline. The company simply couldn't stand another bad year of sales – it was a matter of survival. It was a crash programme. I came up with a good cabinet that year (the 1250) and sales shot up to 14,000 units. I am sure Paul would have been pleased with the design – it was lit up like a Christmas tree but it had subdued colours to make it look like an entertainment machine.

'From 1950 to 1964, I designed all of Wurlitzer's juke box cabinets, wall boxes, speakers and other components. I was never fully happy working under engineering because of the domineering and restrictive attitudes to creativity which got worse as time went on. I made this clear on occasions and they finally terminated my services in October 1964.'

Under the experienced leadership of the new General Sales Manager, A. D. Palmer, Wurlitzer steadily regained composure during the 1950s. Although they never won back the leadership of

*Paul Fuller wall speaker circa 1940 of the ecclesiastic moderne school. (Courtesy Bob Reno)*

the industry, they continued to produce first-class equipment.

Rock-Ola designs in the 1940s were strongly influenced by Paul Fuller's work, but when Wurlitzer lost the leadership of the industry in 1948, Rock-Ola quickly switched its attention to Seeburg products and continued to do so throughout the 1950s. It is hard not to notice the similarity between the 1954 Rock-Ola and the 1952 Seeburg. We must assume that it was a deliberate copy.

AMI, located away from the centre of the industry, had always produced original and interesting designs in their equipment. They weren't all beautiful but at least they were distinctive. In the mid 1950s, their juke boxes were exceptionally strong in appearance, making powerful use of automobile imagery – especially the curved windscreen effect which was straight out of Detroit at that time. With these machines, AMI was able to penetrate the European market with more success than any of its competitors and they have been a big name in the British coin-op business to this day.

Seeburg also drew heavily upon Detroit styles; the automobile was the dominant mechanical artefact in a society which worshipped the machine. However powerful the juke box was as an image source, it was overwhelmed with chromium bumpers, grills, headlights, fins and dashboard features.

To the art historian they might look like caricatures of the car, but at the time they were superb. The soft shoulders and gentle glow of the 1940s had given way to the harsh fluorescent glare, sharp lines and angular metallic shape of the altogether more aggressive machines of the 1950s. The new generation of juke box patrons was younger and angrier than before. Their music was forceful and incoherent and the juke box styles reflected some of these feelings.

During the 1960s, the juke box was effectively ignored by the mainstream of youth culture and it ceased to be the vehicle for popular music that it once was. Its design became more conservative, more subdued, a process which culminated in the 'console'. In order to appeal to an older age-group, the manufacturers tried to eradicate the youthful image of the phonograph, by designing non-juke boxes, or perhaps more accurately, anti-juke boxes.

Predictably, this created a serious problem for the manufacturers; since the console, pleasant, unobtrusive, was keeping a low profile, the public weren't getting bored with it, and the operators were discovering that it could remain in prime locations for twice as long as the juke box. After all, a mahoganite seventeenth-century-style Olde English cabinette with a Gainsborough landscape immortalised on a polyester tapestry is for ever. Although the console kept the industry afloat, especially during the very difficult period in 1973–4, it was, in effect, cutting its own throat. James Sullivan, today's Rock-Ola stylist, explained that this concept fails to incorporate the built-in obsolescence which is essential to a regular turnover of equipment from the public's point of view. The console, being out of the customer's sight, could be retained by the operator for several years and consequently would not need annual renewal.

---

# INDEX

Figures in bold type refer to illustrations of the entries.